LEATHERCRAFT

LEATHERCRAFT

Inspirational Projects for You and Your Home

First published 2016 by
Guild of Master Craftsman Publications Ltd
Castle Place, 166 High Street, Lewes,
East Sussex, BN7 1XU

Reprinted 2018

All projects first published in *Making* magazine

ISBN 978-1-78494-172-7

A catalogue record for this book is available from the British Library.

Publisher: Jonathan Bailey
Production Manager: Jim Bulley
Senior Project Editor: Sara Harper
Designer: Ginny Zeal
Contributors: Emma Herian, Paula Fernandes, Pascale Mestdagh, Jemima Schlee, Jeanne Spaziani, Clair Wolfe
Photography: Anthony Bailey, Emma Herian, Pete Jones, Pascale Mestdagh, Emma Noren, Jemima Schlee, Jeanne Spaziani, Rachel Whiting
Illustrations: Emma Cowley

Colour origination by GMC Reprographics
Printed and bound in China

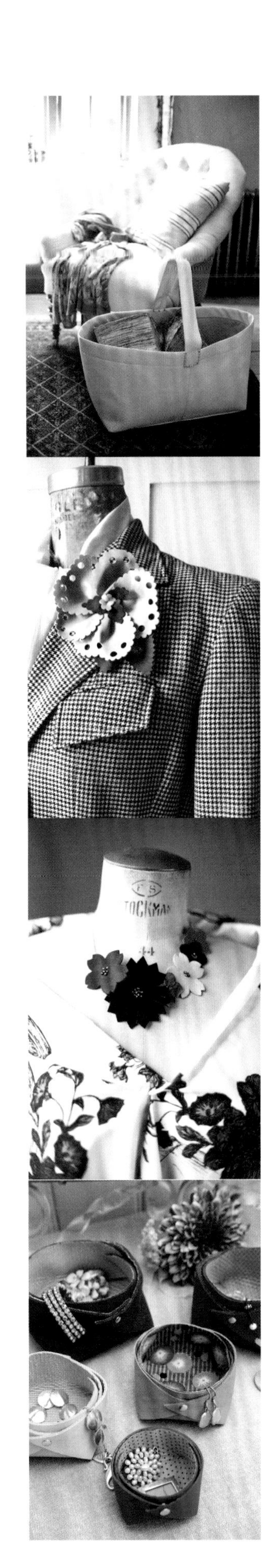

Contents

Introduction

This exciting collection of leather projects, all previously published in *Making* magazine, shows you how to bring a touch of luxury into your life without the hefty price tag. All projects have been selected from the work of gifted designers, so let our talented crafters show you how to create classic leathercraft with a decidedly modern flair.

Whether you simply want to revamp an old belt, make a bag from scratch or create stylish gifts, you'll find plenty of inspiration here. We've divided this book into three handy sections: accessories; bags and purses; and the home. Readers will find fresh and fabulous ideas throughout, including leather necklaces, hand-made booklets, key fobs, iPad covers, and a woven belt chair, plus plenty of bags and belts to give your wardrobe an instant lift.

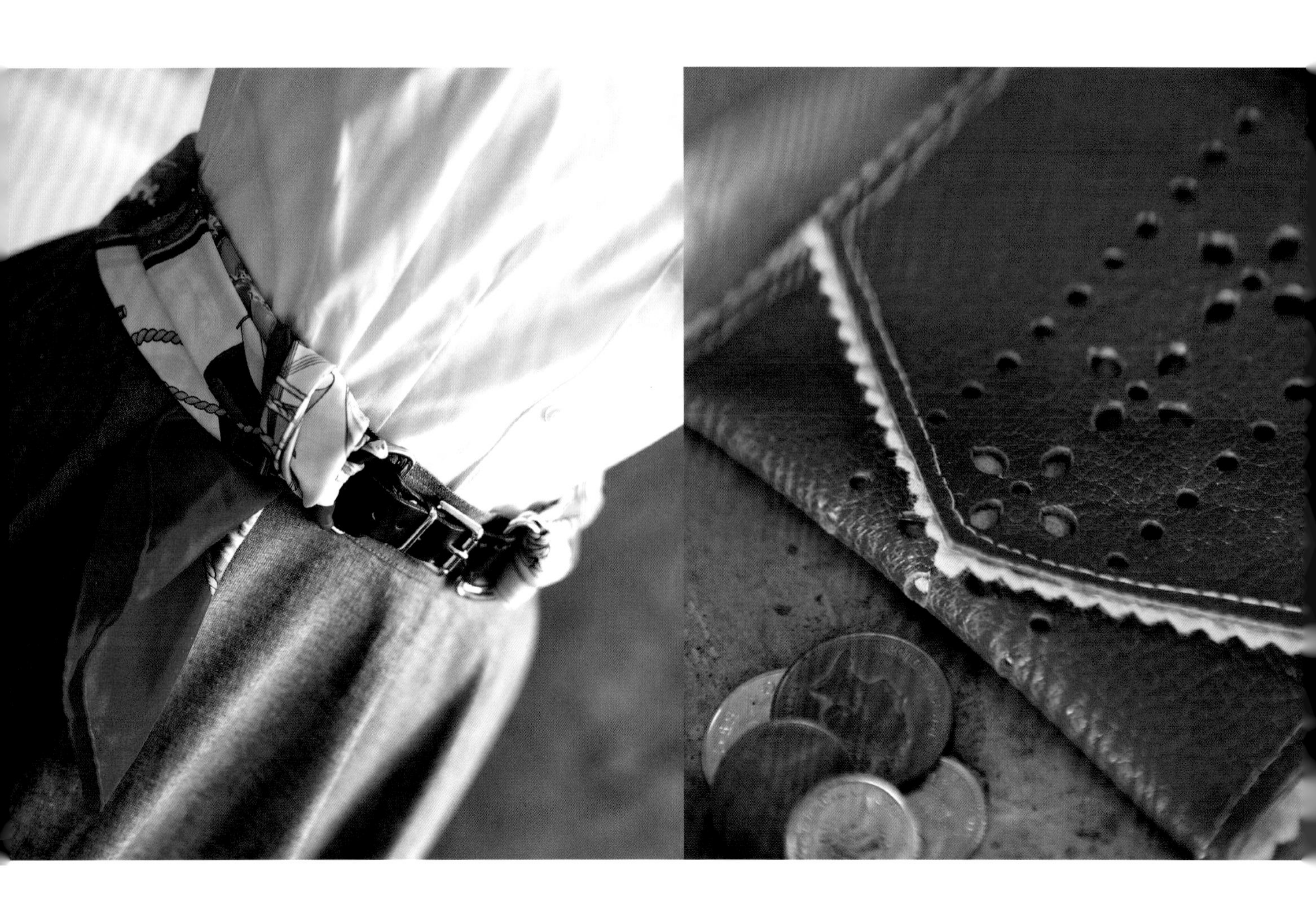

With clear text, colour photographs and detailed illustrations, most projects are suitable for those new to leatherwork, and those of you who already have some experience of the craft are sure to be inspired by the exclusive designs. Even novice leathercrafters will be surprised to find out just how easy it is to make these durable and sophisticated projects. But above all, whatever your level, we're sure you'll have fun making them.

Network
FS
44

Accessories

Friendship bracelet

This macramé bracelet is formed by basic square knotting. It can be made with any number of stringing materials, including leather cord, which may need to be worked a little to make it more supple.

Materials

- Approximately 2½yd (2.3m) of 0.5mm leather cord
- Silver diamond cut decorative jumprings
- Scissors
- Clips or tape
- Embroidery needle
- Glue
- Braiding board or clipboard with a nail in it

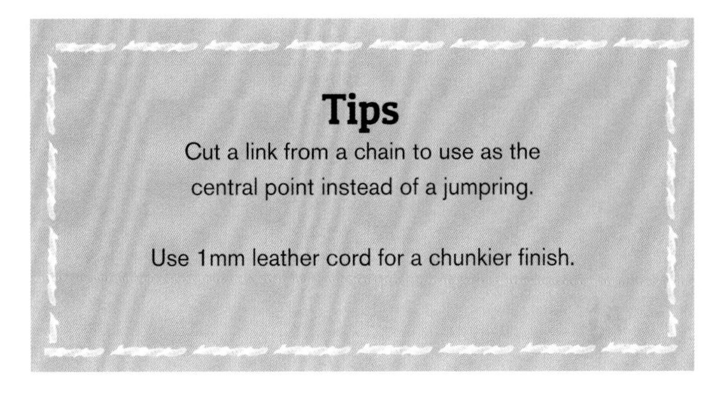

Tips

Cut a link from a chain to use as the central point instead of a jumpring.

Use 1mm leather cord for a chunkier finish.

1 Cut a length of 0.5mm leather cord in your chosen colour and pass it through your fingers several times to make it more supple. Measure and cut two lengths approximately 14in (35.5cm) and two lengths approximately 32in (81cm). Pass one of the shorter lengths of leather cord through a solid jumpring so that the cord is equal lengths on both sides. Use clips or tape to hold in place on the braiding board. A piece of wood with a nail tapped into it will do as well if you don't have a braiding board. Take one of the longer lengths of cord, pass it under the secured cord, centre it, then tie a knot as close to the jumpring as possible. The diagrams show the knotting technique.

2 The square knot is made up of two passes. For the first pass, the left hand strand goes over the central strands and under the right hand strand; this will create a loop.

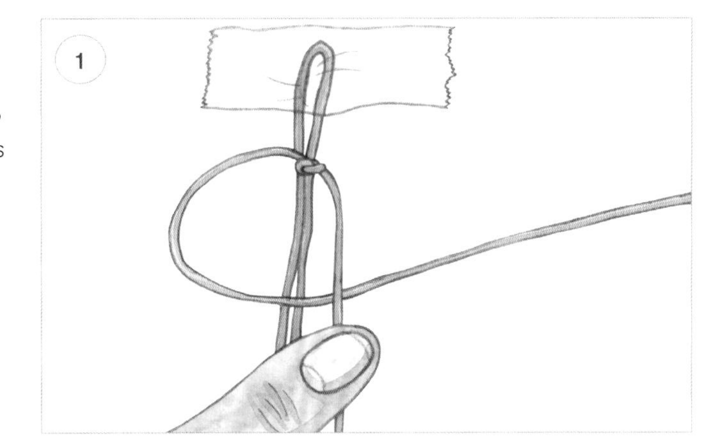

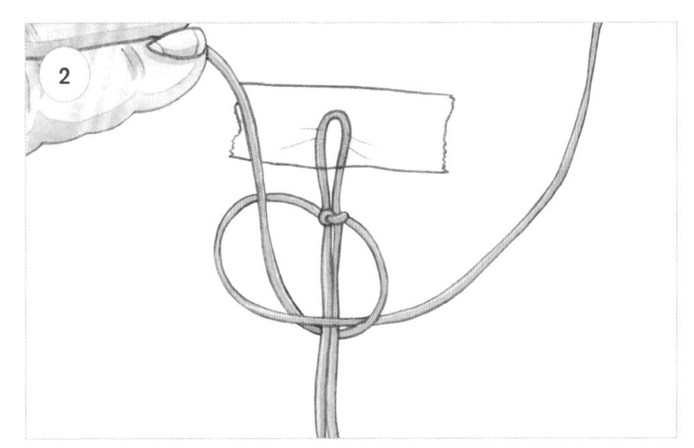

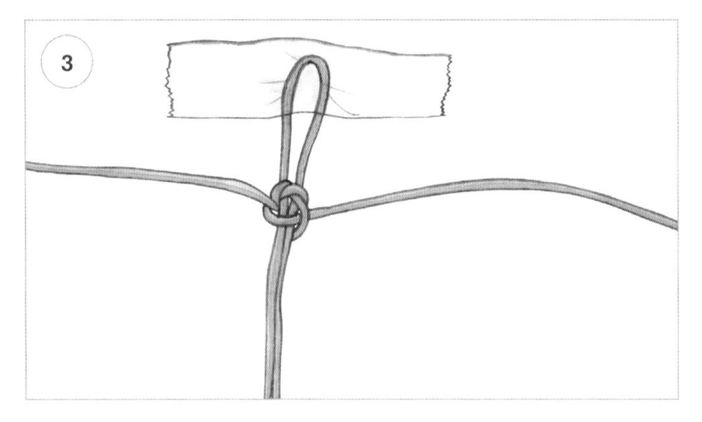

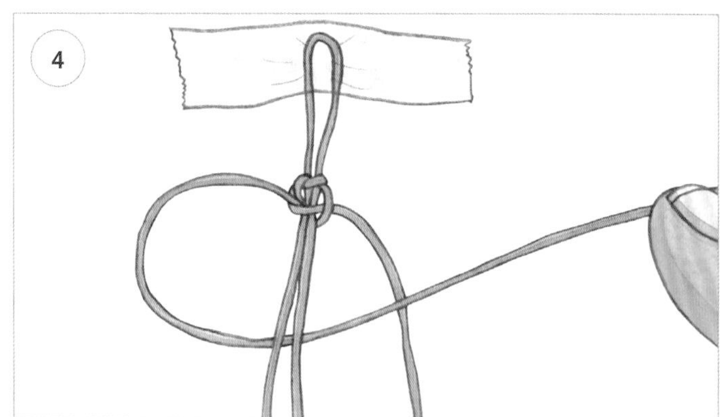

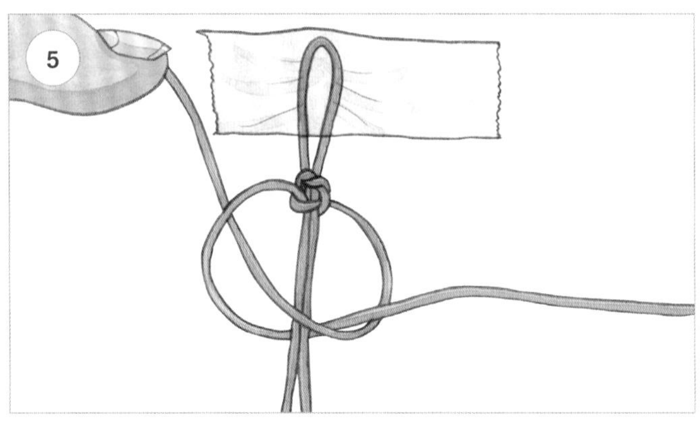

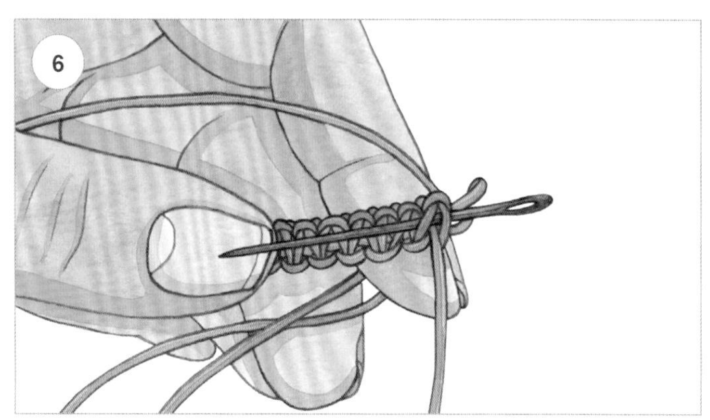

3 The right strand is then passed under the central strands, then up through the loop. Pull both the left and the right strands until the knot is formed, position close to the first knot.

4 For the second pass, to complete a square knot, take the left strand, pass it under the central strands then over the right strand to create a loop.

5 Next, pass the right strand over the two central strands and through the loop. Once again pull tight. Due to the way leather cord is made, there may be weak spots in the strand so do not pull too hard because it may snap.

6 Continue to make square knots until you have about 2in (5cm) of knotting along the central strands. Repeat the above steps on the opposite side of the jumpring. To finish the knots, use an embroidery needle to make a gap under a couple of the knots along the back of the knotting.

7 Pass both the left and right strands through the gap, pull both strands to secure, snip away excess cord then use glue to secure.

8 Once the glue has dried, overlap the middle strands and secure with tape or clips. Use a length of cord to create a short length of square knotting. Do not pull the knots too tightly against the central strands, as there needs to be an allowance for movement. Finish the length of knotting as above; take extra care when applying the glue. Adjust to fit the wrist and tie each of the ends into knots, trimming away any excess.

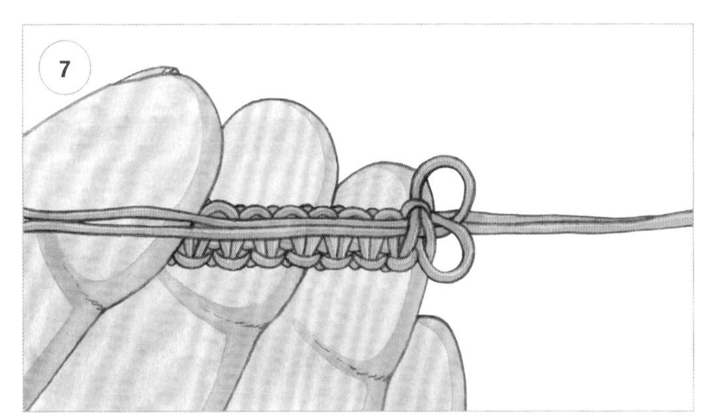
7

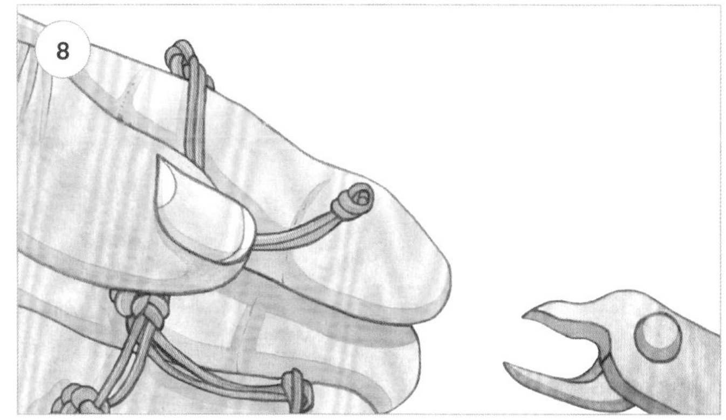
8

Network
15 SEP 14
TO BE CARRIED ON ALL RAIL JOURNEYS.

Luggage tag

This stylish but simple leather luggage tag doesn't require any sewing. Make a matching set or different colours for him and her.

Materials

- 10 x 4in (25 x 10cm) medium weight leather
- 2¾ x 4in (7 x 10cm) plastic transparent credit card sleeve
- 1 snap button and snap button setting tool
- 12–16in (30–40cm) leather shoelace
- Leather punch
- Letter stamps for leather (optional)
- Round corner leather tool (optional)

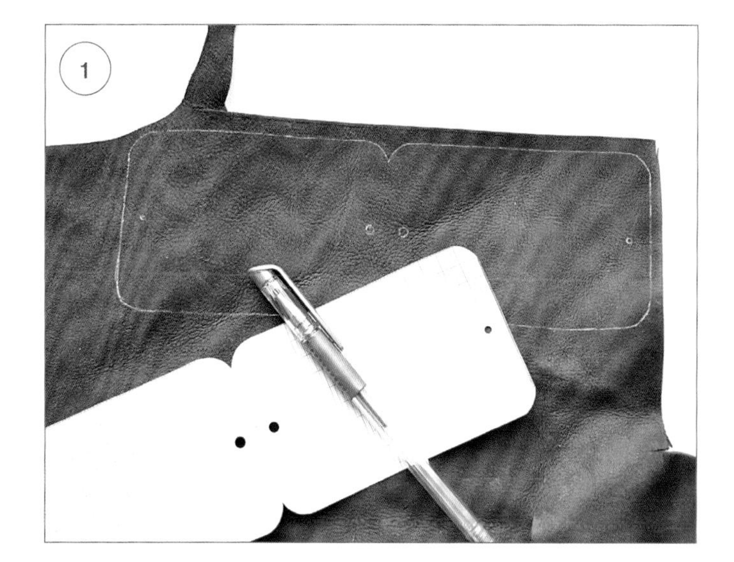

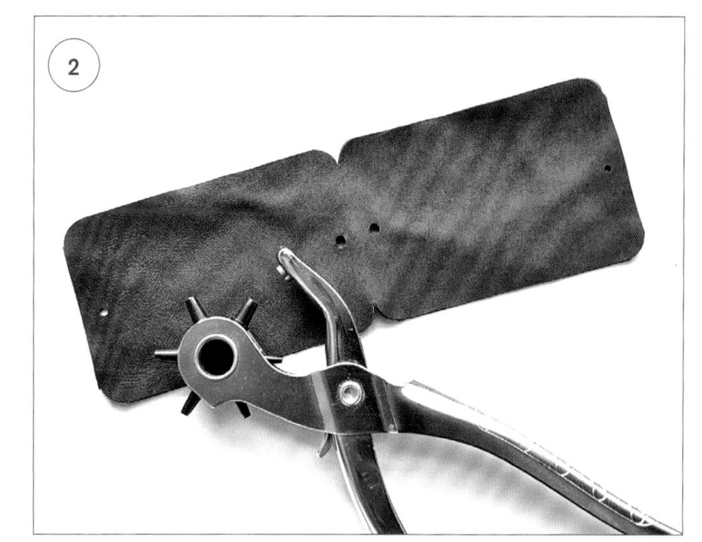

1 Photocopy or trace the template on page 17. If the dimensions of your card sleeve are different, adjust the template accordingly. Make holes in the template for the snap button and strap as indicated. Copy the template onto the wrong side of the leather and mark the holes for snap button and strap.

2 With a leather punch, make holes for the snap button and strap.

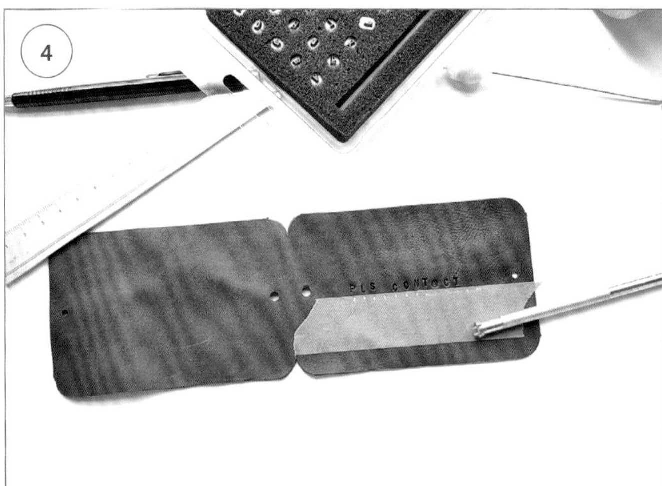

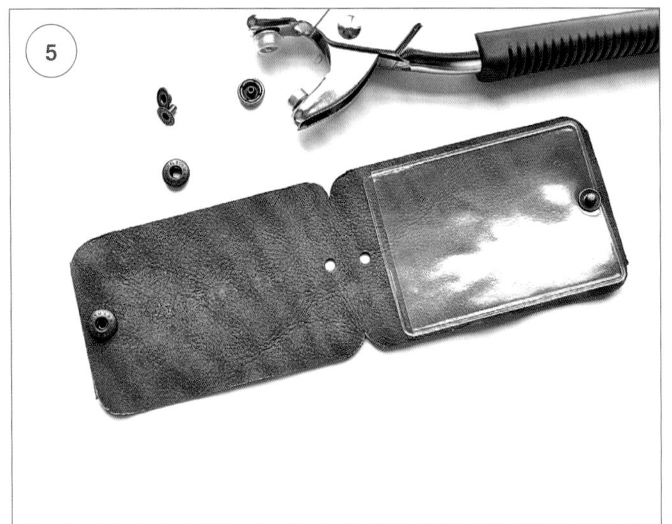

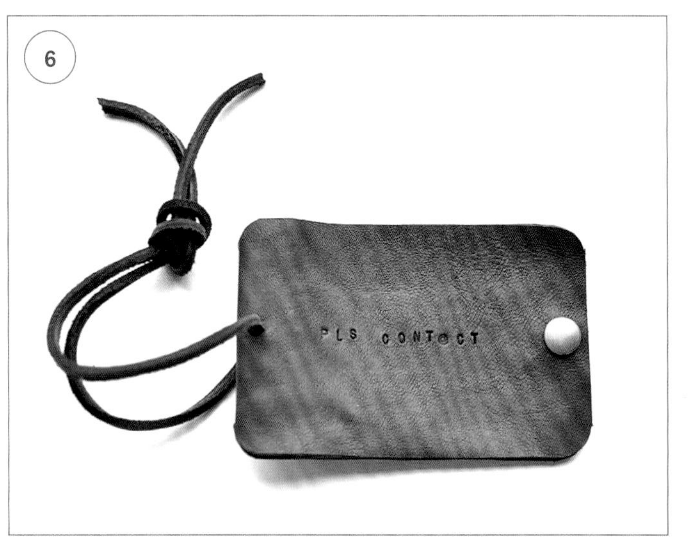

3 Make a hole at the short closed end of the card sleeve, centred and about $\frac{1}{4}$in (6mm) from the edge.

4 To further personalise the tag, add text to the front using special letter stamps for leather (follow the instructions that come with the stamp kit).

5 Set a snap button, making sure to secure the plastic card sleeve under the post of the snap.

6 Fold and snap the tag closed. Thread the leather shoelace through the holes at the top and tie a knot.

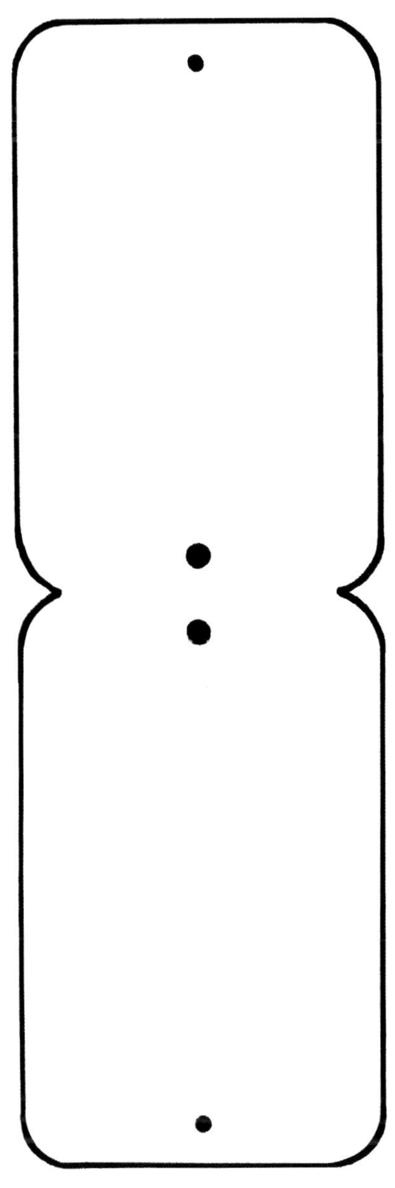

Photocopy at 200%

TEMPLATE

Daisy belt

Make a cute and quirky springtime accessory with this easy upcycle of an existing belt. This charming project is suitable for beginners, and you can use it as inspiration for customizing any number of leather items.

Materials

- Leather belt
- Revolving punch pliers
- Cotton embroidery threads (white, yellow, variegated green/white and variegated pink/white)
- Embroidery needle
- Masking tape
- Scissors

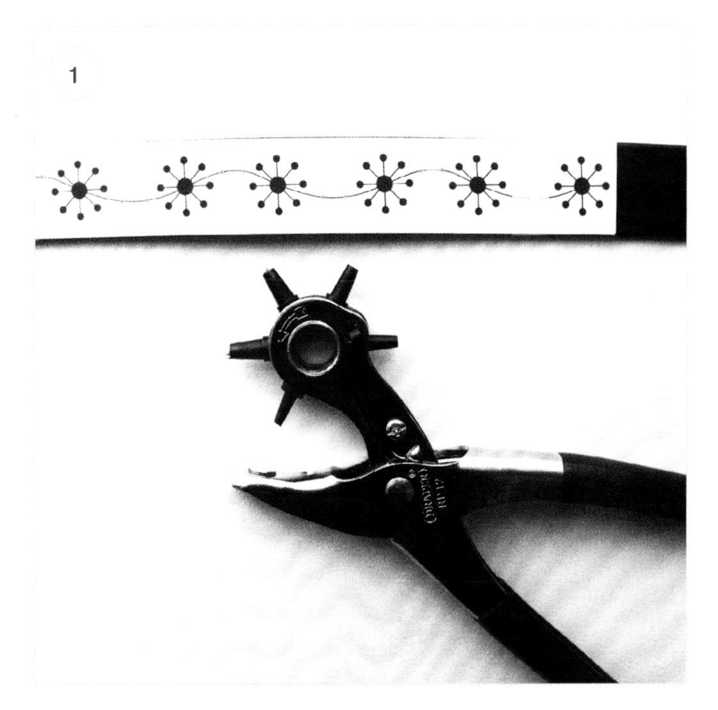

1 Print out the template on page 21 to a size that fits comfortably within the width of your belt. This belt is 1¼in (3cm) wide and the flowers ⅝in (1.5cm) in diameter. Use masking tape to temporarily attach the template to the front of the belt and punch the pattern using $\frac{1}{16}$in (2mm) diameter holes for the outside of the daisies and ⅛in (3mm) holes for the centres. Start 4in (10cm) from the buckle and work along the belt to the other end. Leave out the area around the buckle holes.

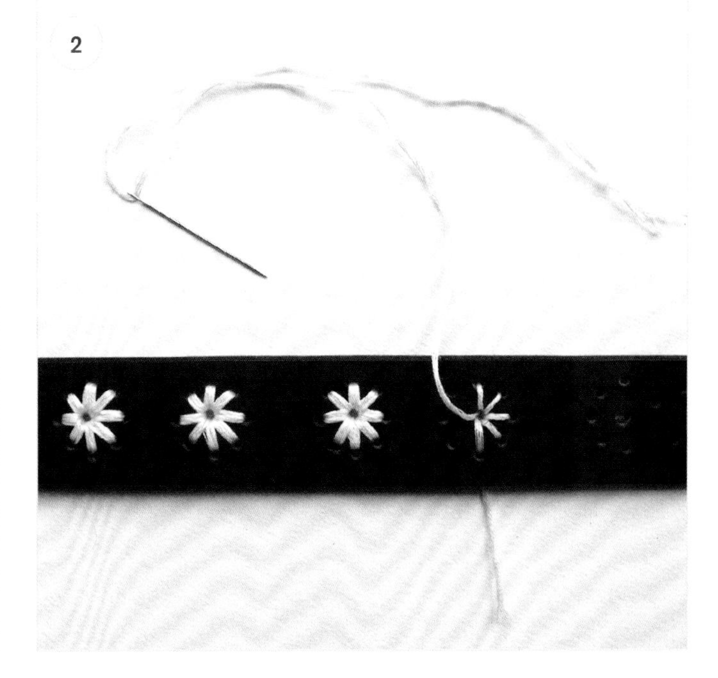

2 Start from one end and stitch each flower. Work around each one three times with white embroidery cotton.

Tip

If the leather punch doesn't make it all the way through the belt on the first go, work over the holes again without the template so that you position the punch accurately over your first effort.

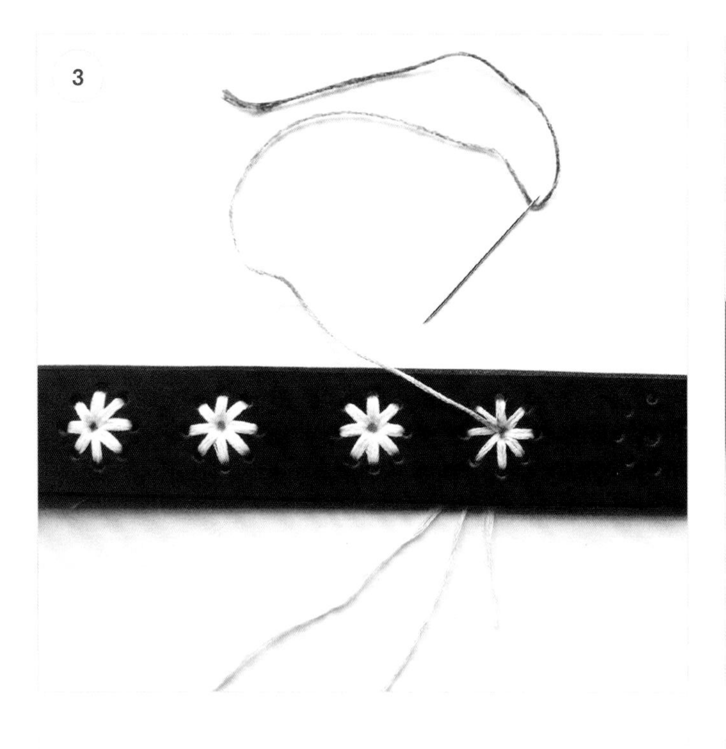

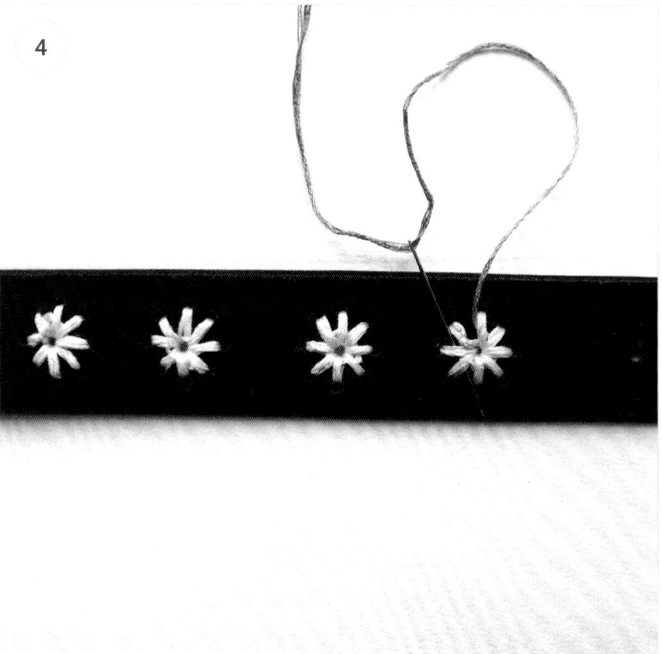

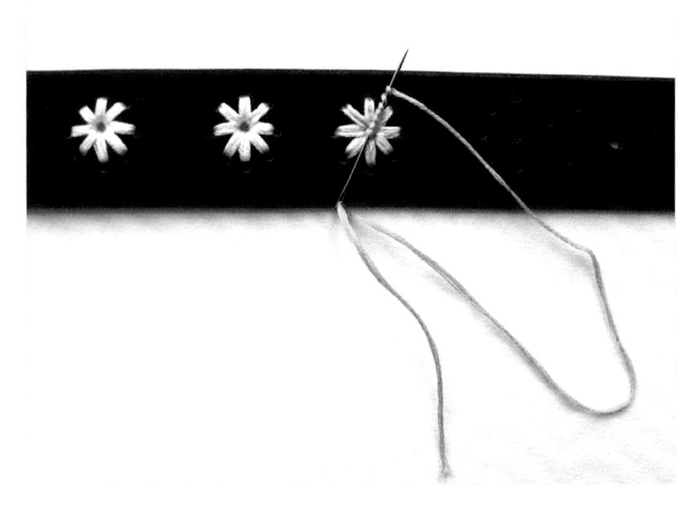

3 On some flowers do two rounds in white and one in variegated pink, positioning the stitches carefully so that the pink thread lies along the centre of each 'petal'.

4 Finish off the threads individually for each daisy by making a few stitches at the back of each flower and running the thread behind the stitching before cutting it.

5 Make the centre of the daisies with a large French knot by wrapping the thread around the needle six times and finish off the thread at the back.

6 Use green variegated embroidery thread doubled to make the 'stalks' – connect each daisy to the next with long stitches at various angles.

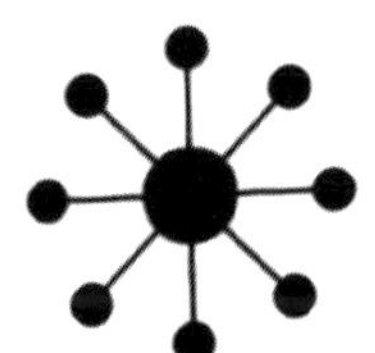

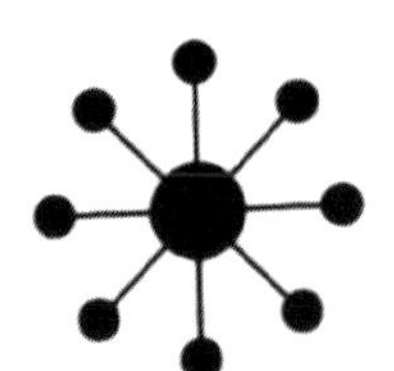

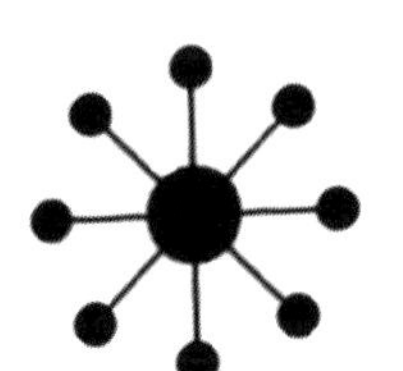

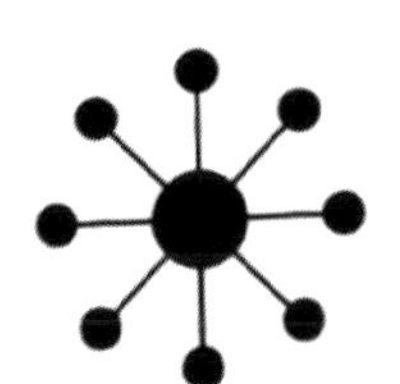

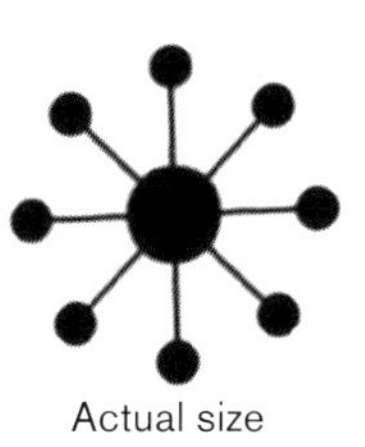

Actual size

TEMPLATE

Glam rock necklace

With an offcut of leather, crystals and glue, you can create a necklace that takes you from desk to dance floor.

Materials

- Offcuts of leather
- Backing material (or more leather)
- Selection of crystals
- Drawing paper
- Greaseproof or tracing paper
- Ruler
- Compass
- Scissors
- Sticky tape or pins
- Cutting board
- Craft knife or scalpel
- Emery paper
- Craft glue
- Chain
- Jumpring and clasp
- Two pairs of pliers

Tips

Look in charity or thrift shops for leather items that can be recycled.

Use ribbon instead of a chain for a quick alternative.

1 Sketch some ideas for the basic bib template on paper. Once you've decided on a design, draw it to size and cut it out. Use greaseproof or tracing paper and a ruler and compass to create the pattern. Cut out the pattern leaving a ⅜in (1cm) border all around.

2 Use sticky tape or pins to temporarily fix the pattern to the leather and place on a cutting board. Using a craft knife or scalpel, carefully cut around the pattern. Repeat this process on backing material or a reversed piece of leather. The two pieces are now ready to be glued. Make sure you are in a well-ventilated room, as the glue fumes can be hazardous.

3 Glue the leather bib template onto some backing material, or another piece of leather, so that the necklace will look neat on the reverse and feel comfortable against your skin. Use a craft knife and scissors to neaten the edges and trim any overlap.

4 Gently rub the surface of the leather over with emery paper – this will create a good surface for the glue to adhere to. Rub harder for a distressed and vintage look. Make sure that the leather is free from dirt and grease before proceeding to the next step.

5 Reuse the paper pattern to plan the design of your crystals. Once the layout is decided, start to stick the crystals onto the leather. Work from the centre out, in a mirroring fashion. Apply a small amount of glue, position the crystal, and then leave it to dry.

6 Finally add a chain so that the necklace can be worn. Fold over the long thin section of the bib, and glue to create a loop. Leave this to dry for at least an hour, and then thread a chain through the loop, and add a jumpring and clasp. Use two pairs of pliers to open and close the jumprings, using a twisting motion.

Silk scarf belt

Give a silk scarf a new lease of life by turning it into an elegant belt, simply by adding a leather buckle and D-rings.

Materials

- Silk scarf
- Leather buckle
- Waxed thread and needle
- 4 x D-rings
- Air-erasable pen
- Scissors
- Panel pin (or any nail with the same diameter as the punched holes in your buckle)
- Hammer

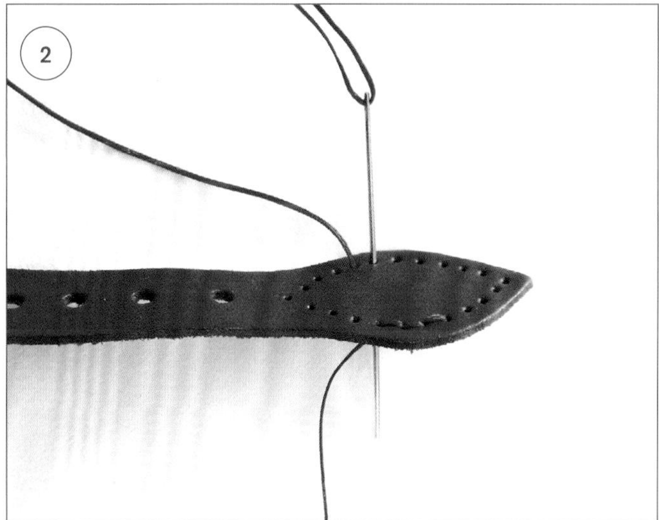

1 Take one half of the buckle and imagine that you have folded over the end punched for stitching back on itself. Use an air-erasable pen to mark extra stitch holes that will be a mirror image of the existing ones, then use the hammer to punch those holes through the leather with the panel pin.

2 With one buckle piece laid down horizontally, complete the three central stitches on the top and bottom edges (blind stitching) through the single thickness of the leather.

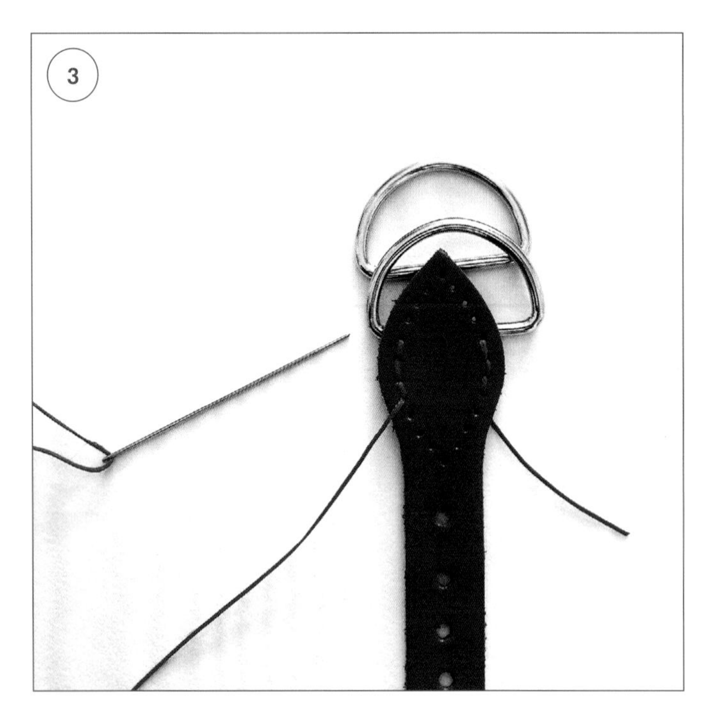

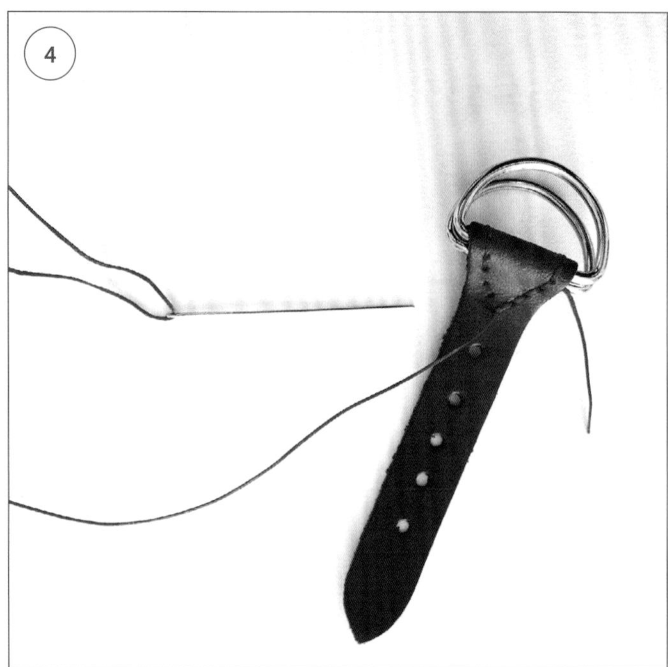

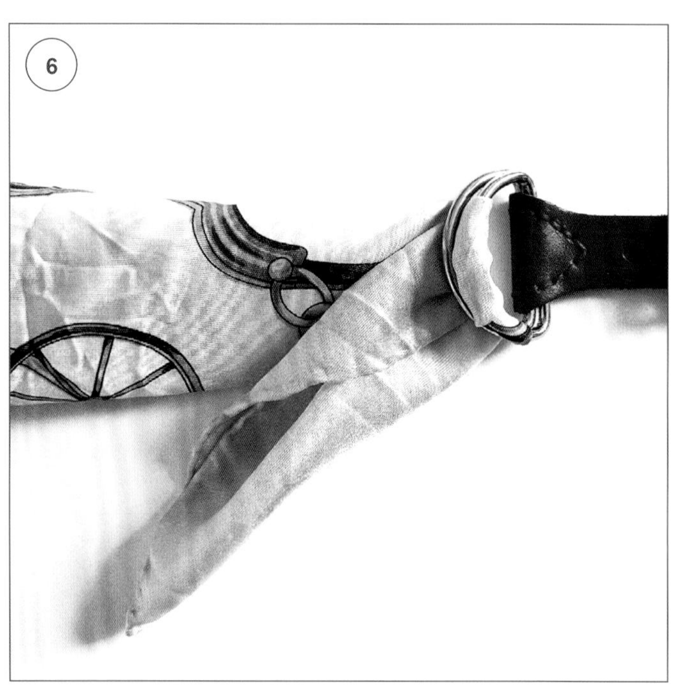

3 Take two D-rings and position so that, when the tip is folded back on itself, they will be encased at the point where you did the blind stitching at step 2.

4 Fold the leather back on itself and over the two D-rings' flat edges. Sew in running stitch following the punched holes from one end to the other and then return, filling in the gaps.

5 Finish off the end of the thread by tying to the other end, trapping the knot between the two layers of leather and then pulling the thread through to the other side of the buckle between the two layers and cutting off tight to the leather edge.

6 Repeat steps 2–5 with the other half of your buckle. Fold the scarf in half diagonally and then fold in on itself to form a long strip. Feed either end into the D-rings.

FS
STOCKMAN
44

Flower necklace

Fashion an eye-catching piece of jewellery from scraps of leather left over from other projects.

Materials

- Scraps of leather or suede large enough for the flowers
- 36 x 4mm beads for flower centres
- 11in (28cm) necklace chain (more if you want a longer necklace)
- 4 x 4mm jumprings
- 3 x 7mm jumprings
- Hook fastening for back of necklace
- Glue
- Small needle-nose pliers
- Leather hand-sewing needle
- Thimble
- Small awl or tapestry needle
- Thread to sew beads on with

Tips

The necklace was made with quite a fine chain, so the smaller 4mm rings were needed as connectors because the larger 7mm ones wouldn't fit directly through the chain links. If your chain has larger links you may not need both sizes of jumprings.

An alternative to using chain would be to simply sew on some pretty ribbon to tie in a bow.

1 Using the paper templates on page 30, cut the three types of flowers out from your suede or leather. If your leather is thin, making the flowers from two layers is a good idea so they will be firm. If this is the case glue two layers of your suede together first then draw around the templates and cut out the required number of flowers. On the large flower (Flower 1) make cuts in towards the flower centre as marked on the pattern piece.

2 Sew clusters of beads in place onto the flower centres using the leather needle and matching thread. The needle-nose pliers can be used to pull the needle through the fabric if it is difficult with just fingers. A thimble would come in handy here, too.

Photocopy all at 100%

TEMPLATES

3 Stitching in between the beads, attach each flower onto one of the two layers of the Flower Base piece, again using the leather needle and thread. After all are sewn, glue the other Flower Base in place to clean finish the back and hide all those stitches.

4 Using the awl or a tapestry needle make one hole through the Flower Base ends as marked on the pattern. Open two of the 7mm jumprings with the pliers and put one through each hole and close them. Open two of the 4mm rings and use them to attach the chain ends to the 7mm rings you just put through the base.

5 Open the length of chain at the centre back and hold up to your neck and check the length. Adjust as needed. Attach the necklace hook to one end using a 4mm ring and attach the third 7mm to the other with the fourth 4mm ring and your necklace is done.

Key fobs

Never misplace your keys again with these handy and practical key fobs. Easy to make, they come in two different styles.

Materials

- Pieces of leather: one piece ¾ x 11in (2 x 28cm) for the outside, two pieces ¾ x 4¾in (2 x 12cm) for the inside
- Sewing threads to match the different coloured leathers
- Sewing machine
- Leather sewing machine needle (optional)
- Sewing needle
- Revolving punch pliers
- Small nickel-plated Sam Browne screw stud
- Scalpel, steel ruler and cutting mat
- 1¼in (3cm) diameter metal keyring
- Two scraps of tissue paper, roughly 2½ x 6in (6 x 15cm)
- Flat-head screwdriver

Tips

Practise sewing through two layers of leather before you start, just to see how your machine copes with the thickness of the leathers. You should have a fairly new, sharp needle but if your leathers are quite soft and not too thick, there is no need to use a leather needle for the machine.

You could line your fob with felt instead of another leather, and use pinking shears to crimp the edges when you trim the inner at step 5.

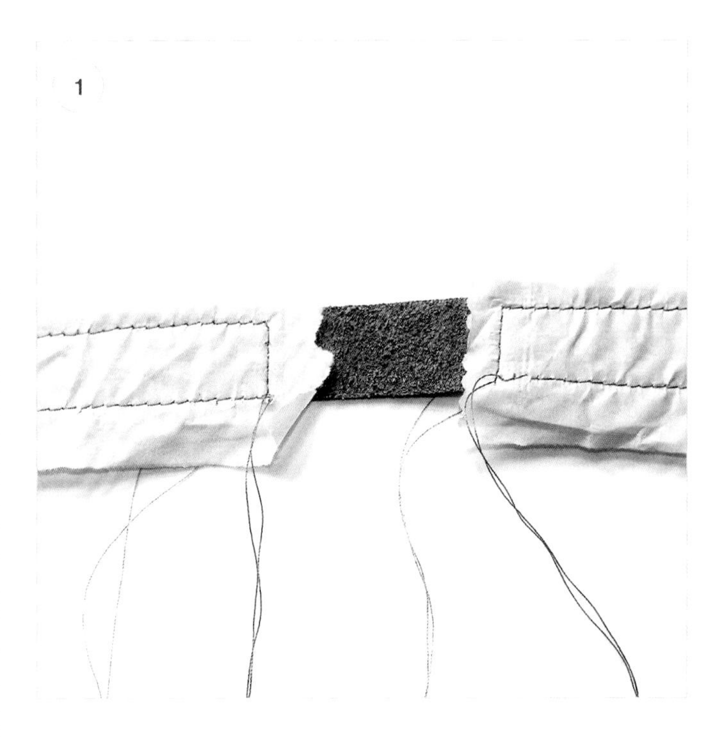

FOR THE FLAT KEY FOB

1 Lay the long outer piece of leather down right side up. Tuck the two inner pieces under each end of it, leaving a 1½in (4cm) gap between them at the centre of the long piece. You will have an excess of the inner leather along the top and bottom and at each end, which will give you leeway for movement when stitching. Now tuck a strip of tissue under each end (this is to help the leather to glide under the sewing machine foot – leather can stick to the machine and fail to pass under the foot).

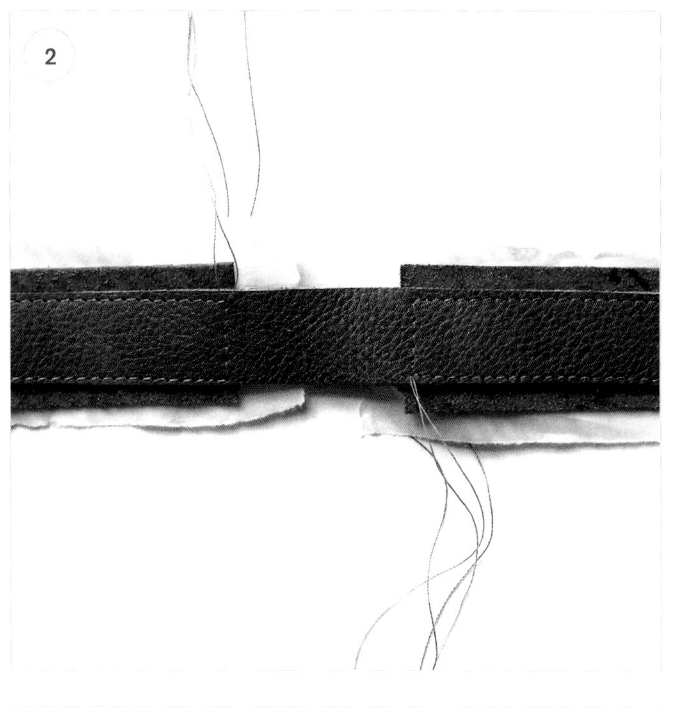

2 Load up the bobbin with thread that matches the inner leather, and thread the machine with thread to match the outer leather.

3 Stitch close to the edge of the leather around each end through both layers (images 1 and 2).

4 Carefully tear off the tissue paper from the underside. Secure the thread ends by threading through a sewing needle and backstitching a few stitches. Snip off any excess thread.

5 Use a scalpel and steel ruler to trim the excess inner leather off to exactly the same size as the outer leather.

6 Fold your strip in half and machine across the width of it three times, just beyond the stitch line of the inner leather to create a channel, so that you are sewing through just two layers of the outer leather. Finish the thread ends off with a sewing needle, and slip a metal keyring through the channel (image 3).

7 Punch a hole the diameter of the Sam Browne screw bit about ¾in (1.75cm) from one end of the strip (through both layers of the stitched inner and outer leathers). Use this hole as a guide to punch a matching hole at the other end.

8 Screw the Sam Browne stud onto one side with a screwdriver with the stud on the inside (image 4).

9 On the other side, cut a ¼in (6mm) slash from the punched hole away from the end with a scalpel (image 5). Connect the Sam Browne stud to the other end by pushing it through the slash.

FOR THE LOOP KEY FOB

10 Repeat steps 1–9, but cut the leather outer to 9in (23cm) and making the inner just 2¾in (7cm) long, keeping the central gap 1½in (4cm) wide at step 1. Connect the Sam Browne stud to the shorter end, with the stud on the outside at step 9.

Rose brooch

This unusual brooch is very quick and easy to make, so is a good project for beginners to the craft.

Materials

- 8 x 8in (20 x 20cm) square of leather
- 5 x 5in (13 x 13cm) square of leather in a contrasting colour
- Decorative edging scissors
- Single hole paper punch or leather punch
- Needle for sewing leather
- Tailor's chalk
- Thread
- Thimble
- Small needle-nose pliers
- Craft glue
- Brooch pin

1 Draw a petal shape on paper, and cut it out. Trace around the pattern onto the back of the leather using the chalk. Cut out five petals using decorative edging scissors (e.g. scalloping or pinking shears). Use a paper or leather punch to make a series of holes close to the outer edge.

2 Fold the base of each petal to form a small pleat, and then add a few stab stitches to hold it in place.

3 Arrange the petals into a rosette, and stitch them in place at the back. When sewing through thick layers of fabric, use a thimble to push the needle in, and a pair of pliers to pull it out again, to save your fingers.

4 Take the contrast leather and cut out three or four small 'inner' petals. Now cut two larger leaves – a piece has been cut out of the centres to make them look more delicate. Return to the original leather, and cut out a small circle to form the centre of the rose.

5 Thread the leather needle with double thread and sew the inner petals and flower centre in place.

6 Turn the flower over and secure the leaves at the back with a few stitches.

7 Still using the leather needle, sew a brooch pin to the back of the flower.

8 Cut another small circle of the original leather, and glue it over the brooch base. This will make the finish neater, and strengthen the bond.

Leaf belt

This sweet and simple leather belt will complete any outfit.

Materials

- 10in (25cm) soft brown leather
- Ornate buckle
- Leather hole punch tool
- Extra strong thread
- Sewing machine with a leather needle
- Scissors

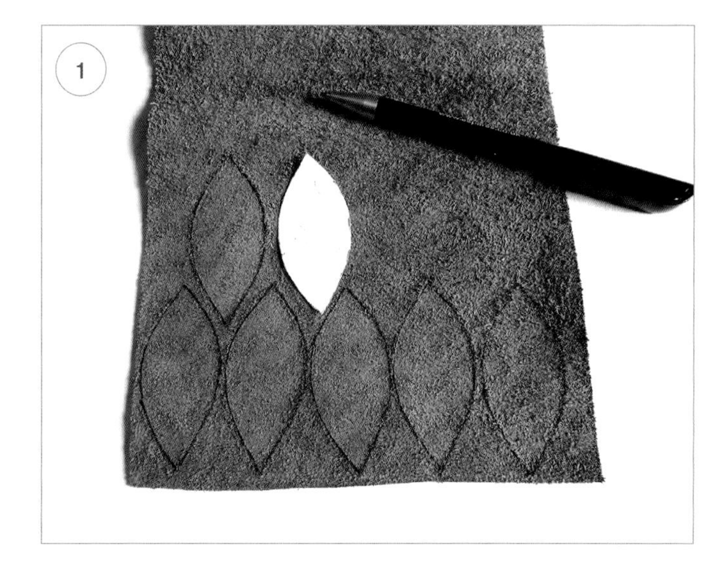

Tips

Test the leather through your sewing machine first and see which stitch is suitable.

Use a different leaf shape and mix it up with other colours of leather.

1 Using the leaf template on page 41, draw out around 35 leaves onto the reverse of the leather, then cut each one out and put to one side.

2 Take the buckle and cut a 3in (8cm) length of leather to the width of the inside of the buckle.

3

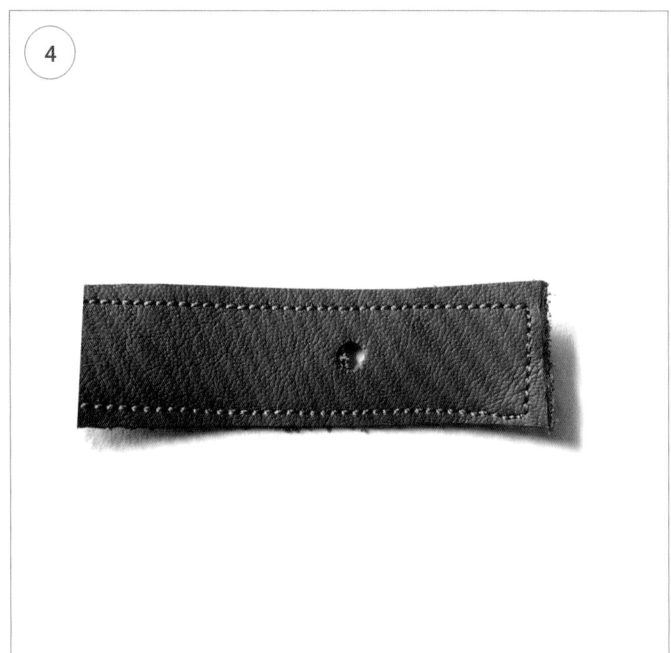
4

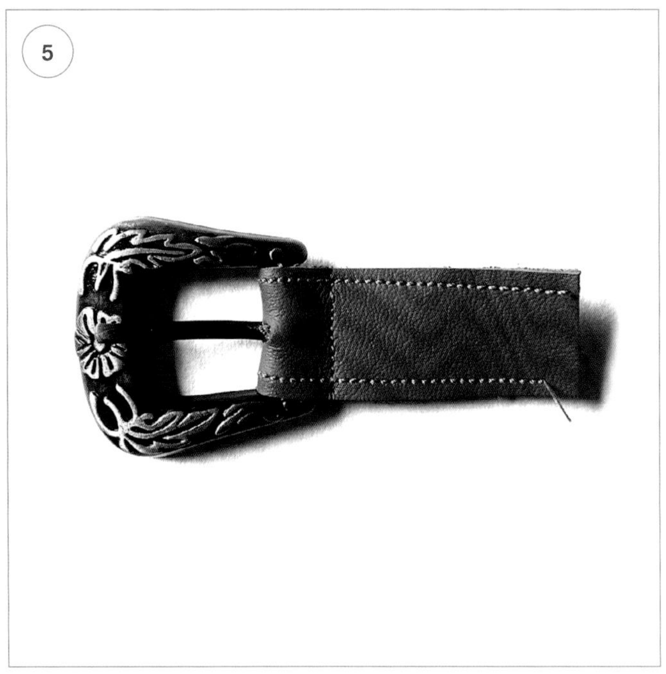
5

6

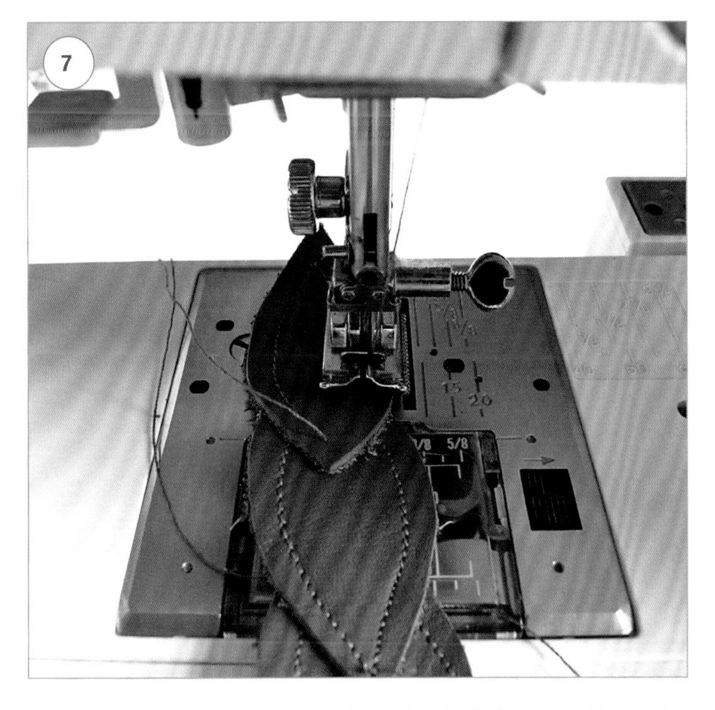

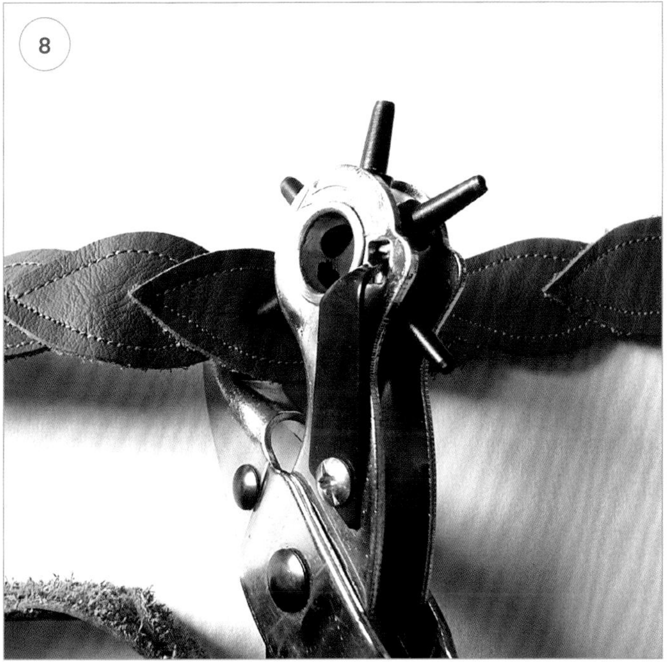

3 Using the leather hole puncher, make a large hole 1¼in (3cm) in from one end.

4 With the sewing machine and strong thread, sew a running stitch hem ⅜in (1cm) from the edge all the way around the strap and neaten off loose threads).

5 Place the strap through the buckle so that the pin goes through the hole and the shorter end of the strap is facing the back. Sew across the width of the strap with a running stitch to hold the buckle in place and neaten off any threads.

6 Take one of the leaves cut in step 1 and place on the front of the strap so that the tip of the leaf is roughly 1¼in (3cm) from the buckle pin. Using the sewing machine, carefully sew the leaf in place using a ⅜in (1cm) hem running stitch all the way around the edge of the leaf, sewing across the width too. Neaten off any loose threads to the reverse of the belt.

7 To attach the remaining leaves, simply sew each one into place so that the tip of each leaf sits to the centre of the leaf below. Sew using a running stitch around the edge in a leaf shape and neaten off the loose threads to the reverse of the belt.

8 Once all the leaves have been sewn to the desired length (add more if needed) wrap the belt around your waist and mark on the reverse where you need to make the holes. Then selecting the large hole on the hole puncher, punch between two leaves where there is only one layer of leather to go through.

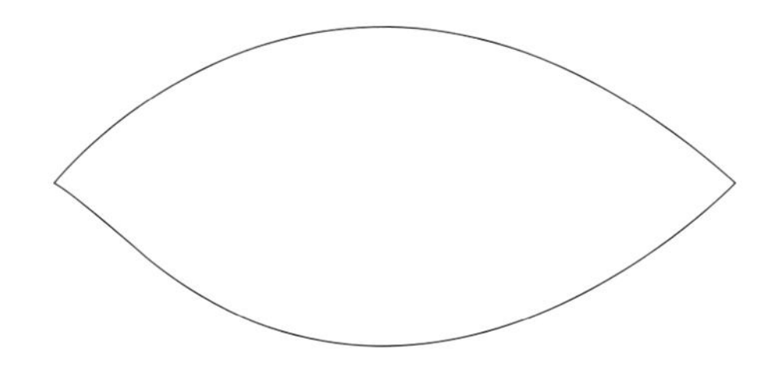

Photocopy at 100%

TEMPLATE

Bags & purses

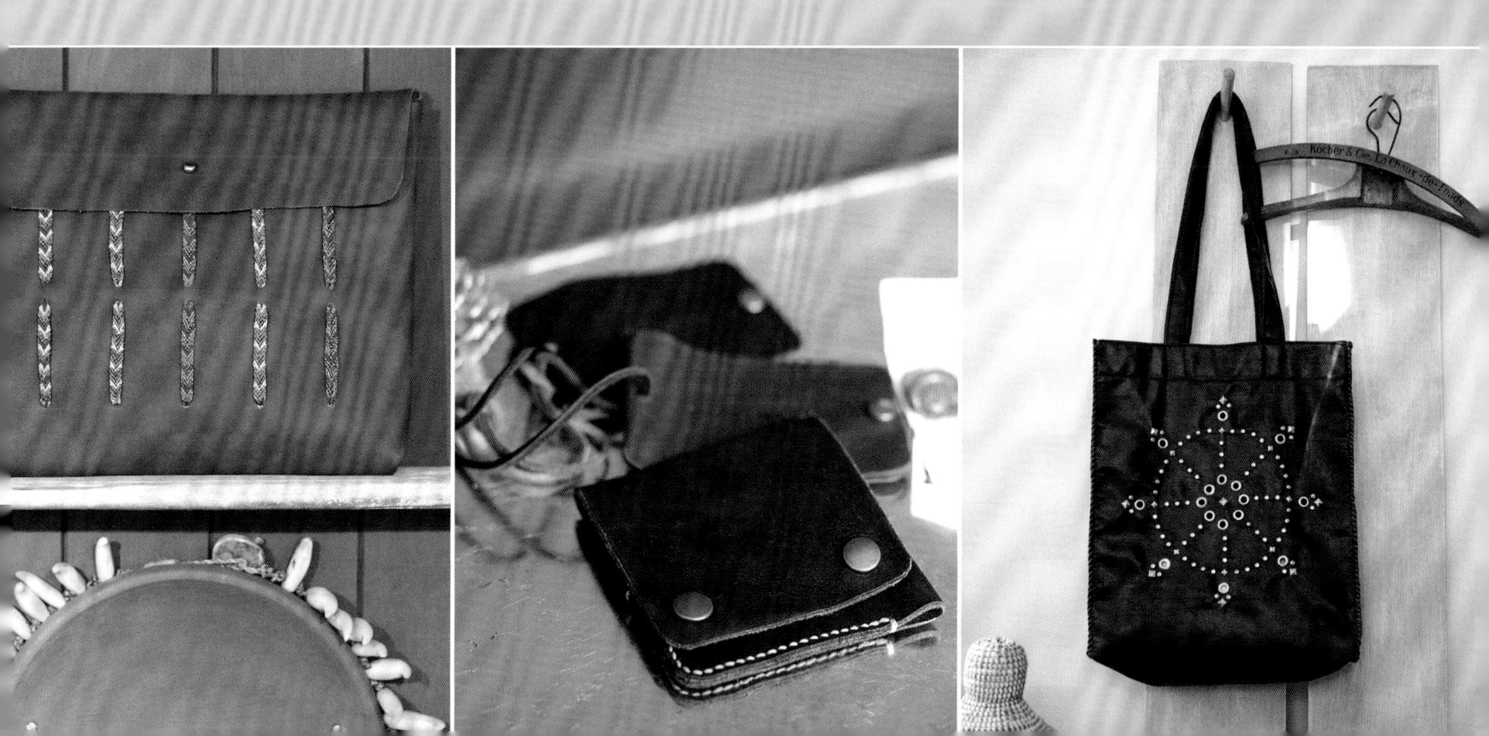

Hand-sewn bag

Basic hand sewing skills are all you need to make this very simple yet stylish leather bag.

Materials

- Half hide of leather (about 27sq ft/2.5m^2)
- Approximately 2⅛yd (2m) x ¼in (5mm) wide leather cording, for straps
- Leather punch
- Pricking iron or stitching awl
- Wooden or rubber hammer
- Heavy-duty thread, waxed linen or nylon
- 2 heavy-duty sewing needles
- Craft glue
- Magnetic snap
- Rotary cutter
- Cutting mat
- Ruler
- Pen
- Beeswax to wax sewing thread (optional)

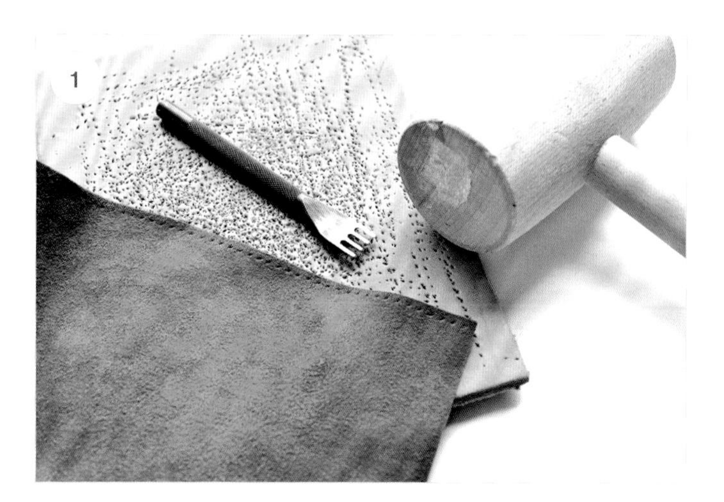

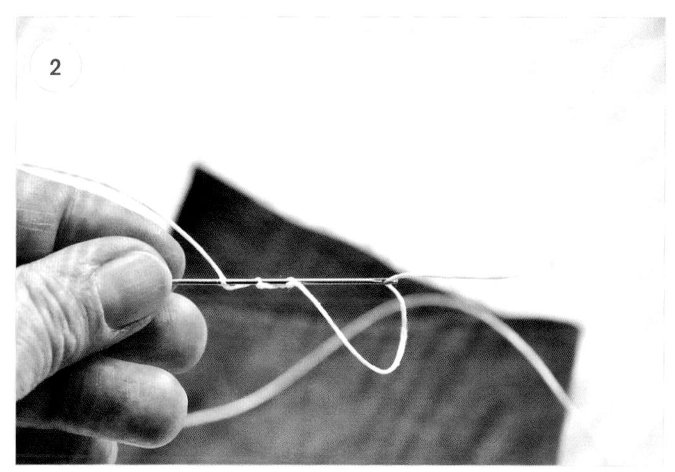

BEFORE YOU START

Cut a 16 x 32in (40 x 80cm) rectangle for the body of the bag, or two rectangles of approximately 16 x 16in (40 x 40cm) each if the hide doesn't allow for working in one piece. Cut six x 2in (5cm) squares and put aside.

1 Make stitching holes for the side seams (and the bottom seam, if applicable) using a pricking iron or awl and ruler, about ¼in (5mm) from the sides. When using an awl the size of the stitches shouldn't be any longer than about ⅛in (3–4mm).

2 Cut a piece of thread approximately 2⅛yd (2m) long (or roughly five times the length of one side seam) and thread a needle at each end. Lock the needles by pulling the threaded needle through the thread a couple of times at short intervals.

3 Pull the threaded needle through the first stitching hole until there is an equal length of thread on both sides. Make a couple of stitches through the first hole and over the top.

4 Sew the side seam using a saddle stitch (see page 63). Push the first needle through the first open hole – you now have two needles on the same side of the work.

5 Take the other needle and push it through the same hole you just pulled the first needle from. You should have one needle on each side of your work again.

6 Push the needles in opposite directions through the same opening. Repeat this all the way down. At the end of the seam, lock by working your way back up again over a couple of stitches, using the same saddle stitch technique. Tie a knot and cut off both ends. You can use a small dab of glue to secure the knot. Repeat for the other side seam (and bottom seam, if applicable), starting out with a new strand of thread.

7 Take two of the squares cut earlier and attach the male and female part of the magnetic snap to them.

8 Next, generously apply glue to the back of the magnetic snap squares and glue them into place, onto the wrong sides of the bag, perfectly in the middle and about ⅜in (1cm) from the top. To make sure the glue adheres, lightly hammer the squares. Dab away any excess glue and leave to dry.

9 Determine where you want the straps to sit. Then, position and glue into place each of the four remaining squares, about ⅜in (1cm) from the top, on the wrong side of the leather. These will reinforce the leather where the strap holes are. Hammer lightly, dab away excess glue and leave to dry. Mark the centre of each square and punch a hole with the leather punch. Repeat for the other squares.

10 Cut the leather cord to size to make two straps for the bag. Tie a double knot at one end, thread through the hole, thread through the other hole and finish off with another double knot. Repeat for the second strap.

3

4

5

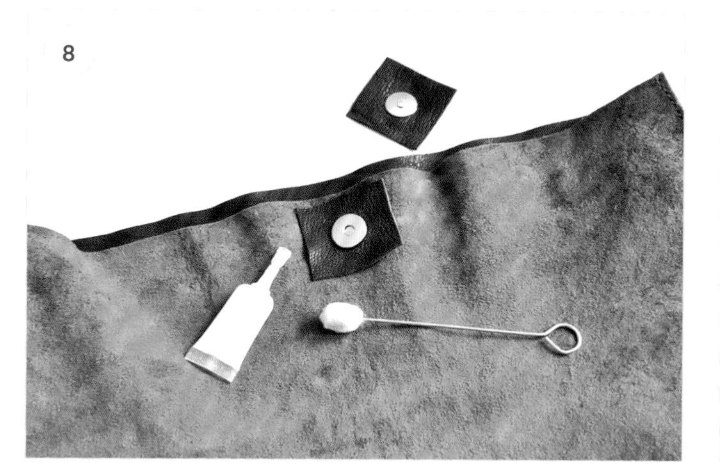

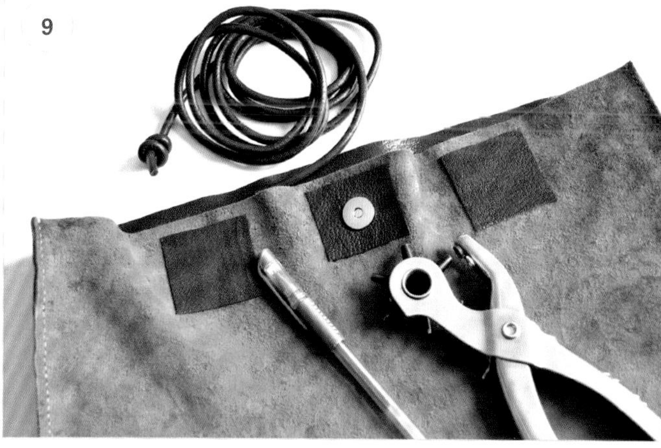

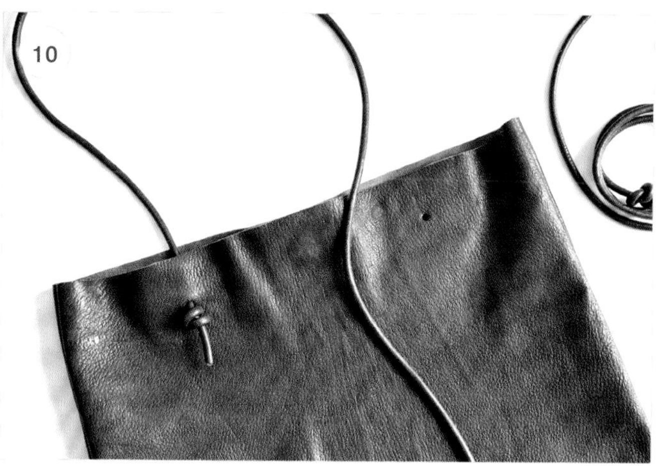

Tips

You can use solid beeswax to make your thread more slippery to avoid knotting and twisting.

If you used a pricking iron you will notice that the holes are slightly slanted. To get a nice and even stitch line, make sure to always stitch at the same angle, i.e. to always push the second needle behind the stitch made by the first.

Purse and wallet

Make a matching purse and wallet
in brightly coloured leather.

Materials

- 8 x 12in (20 x 30cm) of leather in colours of your choice
- Matching extra strong thread
- Sewing machine with leather needle
- Pen
- Ruler
- Scissors
- Button
- Scalpel
- Leather punch

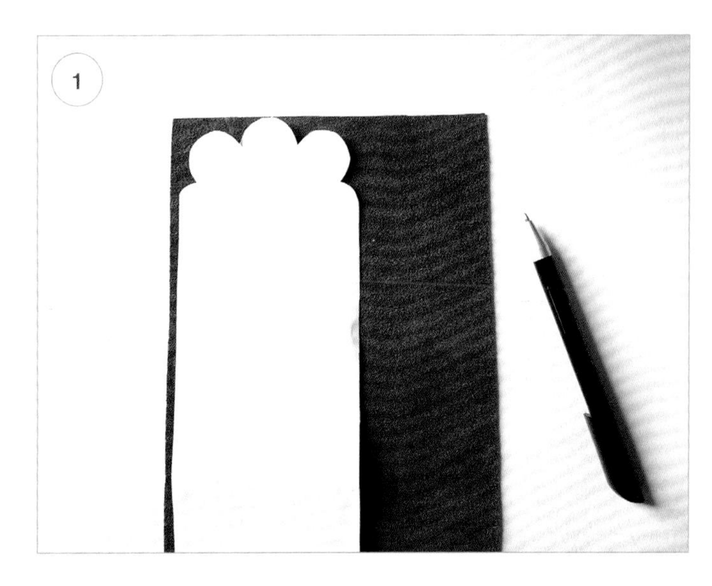

PURSE

1 Using the purse template on page 51, cut out and draw around onto the back of the leather, then cut it out. Cut a strip of the same leather about ⅝in (1.5cm) wide and slightly longer than the width of the purse. With your sewing machine and the extra strong thread sew all the way around the strip with a ¼in (5mm) running stitch hem. Put to one side.

2 On the reverse of the leather mark 3½in (9cm) up from the bottom and then again 3½in (9cm) from that point – do this either side of the purse.

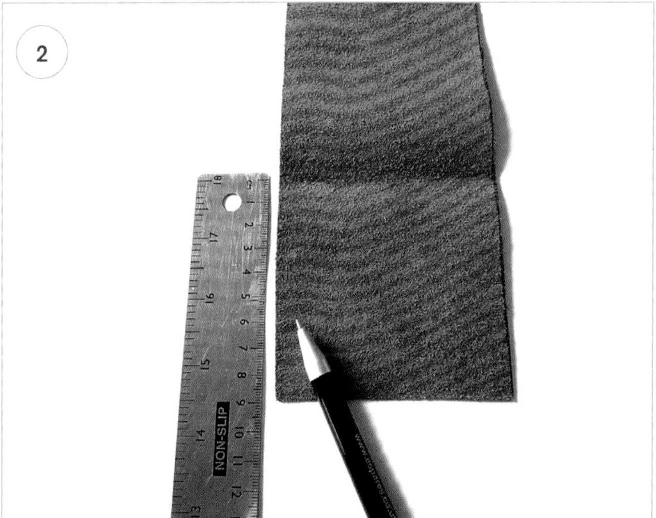

Tips

Have fun with the shape of the flap using different sized leather punches to create various patterns.

Make sure you use a leather needle on your sewing machine.

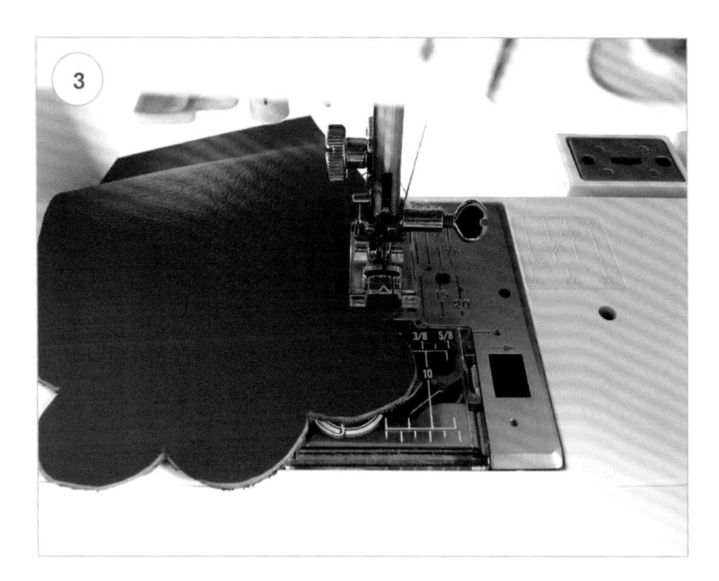

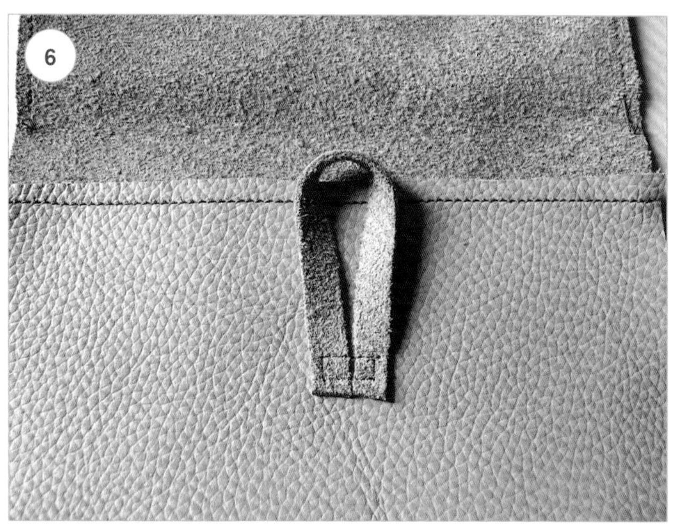

3 Using the matching thread on your sewing machine, and starting from the second 3½in (9cm) mark, sew around the top edge of the purse with a 5mm running stitch hem making sure you backstitch either end and neaten off stray threads.

4 Fold the leather up from the first 3½in (9cm) mark to the second, then place the strip cut in step 1 roughly around 1¼in (3cm) from the top 3½in (9cm) mark. Sew down either side of the purse so that the strip and edges are all sewn together. Backstitch either end and neaten off any stray threads with a needle.

5 Using the leather punch, cut a small hole in each of the scallops to give a pretty ornate edge, then simply close the purse by placing the flap under the strip.

WALLET

1 Using the wallet template on page 51, follow steps 1 and 2 as for the purse, but cut a ⅓ x 4¾in (8mm x 12cm) strip of leather to make the fastening.

2 Sew a similar hem along the ornate top edge of the wallet using the matching thread (as in step 3 for the purse) as well as the straight edge.

3 Take the thin strip of leather and fold in half, position as a loop in the middle, about 2in (5cm) from the straight edge and sew in place neatening off any threads (image 6). Sew a button just below this loop, making sure it is attached securely.

4 Sew down either side of the wallet and neaten off any stray threads. Finally, with the scalpel, make a small slit in the middle of the flap, thread the leather loop through the slit and twist over the button to secure the flap.

TEMPLATES

Purse

Wallet

Photocopy at 250% for actual size

Drawstring pouch

Use vintage or recycled leather for this easy no-sew project and make a gorgeous leather coin pouch, perfect for carrying loose change or keepsakes.

Materials

- Square of leather about 8 x 8in (20 x 20cm), approximately ⅛in (3mm) thick
- 2 x 20in (50cm) lengths of thin, strong leather cord
- Scissors (strong enough to cut leather)
- Black marker pen
- Leather puncher or sharp paper-hole puncher

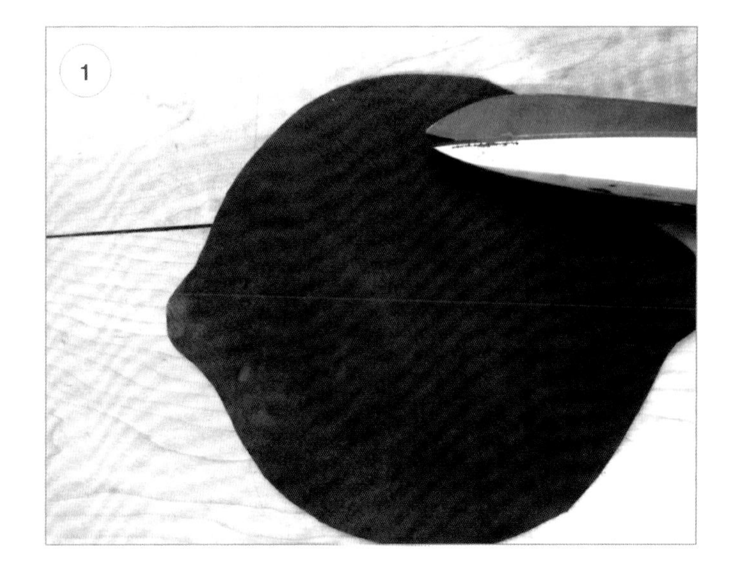
1

Tips

Before threading the leather cord, test its strength by pulling at it to make sure it does not break.

To find a leather square of about 8 x 8in (20 x 20cm), you could use an old bag or jacket. The older the leather, the better the pouch will look. You can also buy leather from craft shops, markets and online.

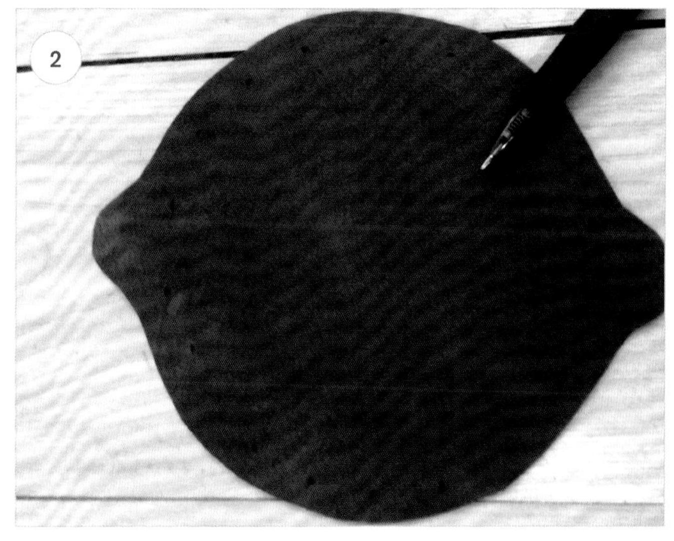
2

1 Stretch out the leather and, if necessary, iron out any creases by placing heavy books or magazines on it for a few hours.

2 Photocopy the template on page 55 at 200% to get to the correct size (7 x 6in/18 x 15cm). Use this to mark out the lemon shape on the leather.

3 Now use scissors to cut out the lemon shape (image 1).

4 With the marker pen, mark twenty dots about ⅜in (1cm) apart around the circumference of the leather shape, about ¼in (6mm) from the edge of the pattern (image 2).

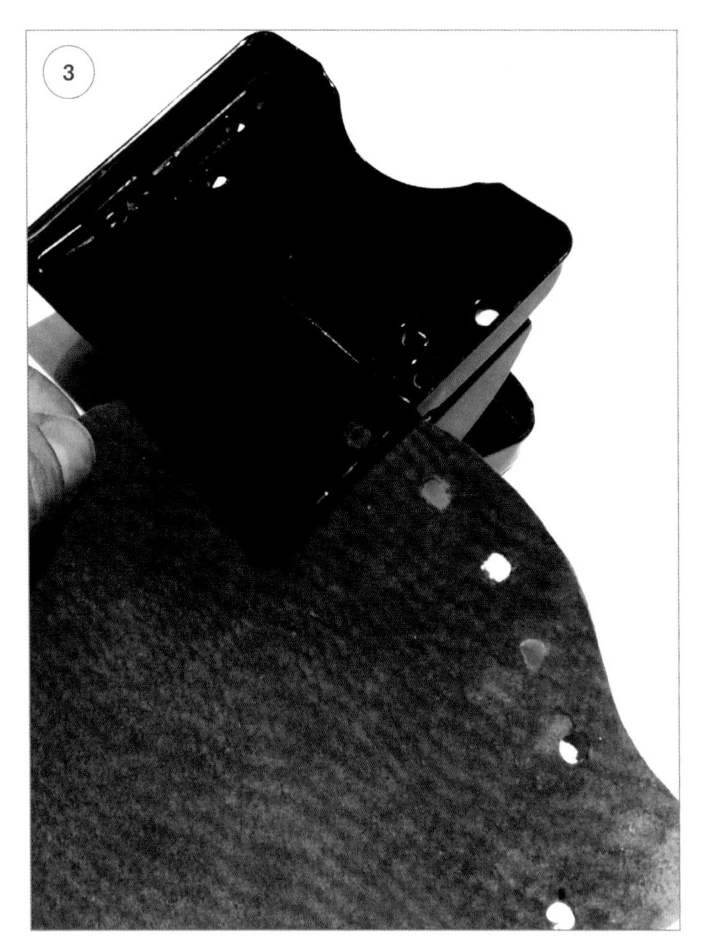

5 Use the leather puncher to punch holes on to the dots. If you are using a hole puncher, use it open and upside down (image 3).

6 You are now ready to thread the first cord length through. Start at one end of the lemon 'head' and go all the way to the other side, using all the holes.

7 Now do the same with the second cord length, threading the cord from the opposite lemon 'head'.

8 You should now have two ends of the cord coming out of each side of the lemon heads (image 4).

9 Tie a double knot on all four ends of the two cords and pull in opposite directions.

Photocopy at 200% to make a pouch measuring 7 x 6in (18 x 15cm)

TEMPLATE

Belt purse

Make a traditional soft leather coin purse, with a handy belt loop. If you can only find small scraps of leather, patch them together to make the finished size.

Materials

- 6 x 10in (15 x 25cm) soft leather
- 4in (10cm) metal zip
- 5 x 9½in (13 x 24cm) printed cotton fabric, for lining
- Thread to match the leather
- Leather sewing machine needle
- Sewing machine
- Zipper foot
- Scissors
- Tissue paper
- Rotary cutter (or scalpel)
- Cutting mat
- Ruler

1 Trim the leather to a rectangle measuring 5 x 10in (13 x 25cm) using the rotary cutter or scalpel. From the scraps, cut a rectangle ¾ x 3¼in (2 x 8cm). Cut the lining fabric to 5 x 9½in (13 x 24cm).

2 Place one short end of the leather right side up on a strip of tissue paper. Position the zip upside down centrally along the short edge and sew by machine using a zipper foot.

Tip

Using tissue paper stops the leather sticking to your sewing machine.

3

4

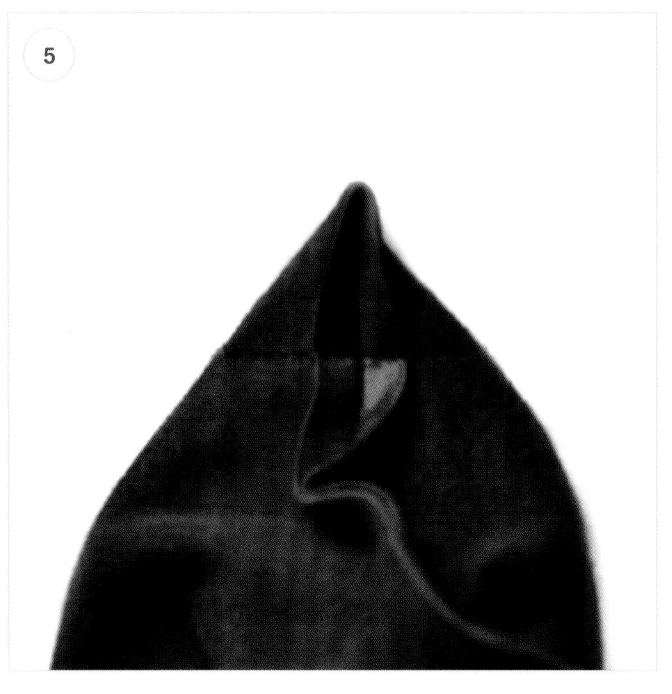
5

6

3 Tear the tissue away and fold the other short end of the leather around to line up with the other side of the zip. With the wrong side out, stitch the zip to the leather, again backing it with tissue to help it move smoothly through the machine. You now have a tube of leather joined by a zip.

4 With the leather 'tube' inside out and the zip open, position the lining rectangle right side down over the zip and leather so that the two short edges align. Stitch in place by machine through all layers. Take the other short edge of the lining rectangle and align it with the other side of the zip and stitch by machine.

5 Now pin the folded long edges of the lining fabric, right sides facing, and sew one side from zip end to folded end by machine. Do the same with the other side, but just half way down from the zip to the fold – this will leave you a gap for turning out. You will end up with what looks like two separate tubes. Take the small leather rectangle and stitch a couple of millimetres in from either long edge to help it hold its shape. Stitch the full length of the two sides of the leather, from the zip to the fold, inserting the folded leather rectangle in one seam ⅝in (1.5cm) below the zip (make sure you do this with the zip at least half open). Stitch across the bottom corners of the leather at a 90-degree angle, ¾in (2cm) from the point.

6 Do the same with the bottom corners of the lining. Turn the purse through the gap in the lining so that it is leather side out and use slip stitch to close the gap in the lining seam.

Fringed bag

Discover how easy it is to make a handbag with this simple hand-sewn project. Suede is the most suitable material for this bag.

Materials

- Leather in the following measurements:
- Front panel: nubuck, 8½ x 11½in (22 x 29cm)
- Back panel and flap: suede, 8½ x 25in (22 x 63cm) when working in one piece (see below) or 18 x 14in (46 x 35cm) when working in two pieces
- Pocket (optional): leather (any type), 5 x 6in (13 x 16cm)
- Leather cording: 5¾yd (5.25m), cut into three
- Pricking iron or stitching awl
- Wooden or rubber hammer to use with pricking iron
- Heavy-duty thread, waxed linen or nylon
- 2 heavy-duty sewing needles
- Rotary cutter and scissors
- Cutting mat
- Ruler (quilter's grid ruler if available)
- Pen
- Double-sided removable tape
- Beeswax to wax sewing thread (optional)

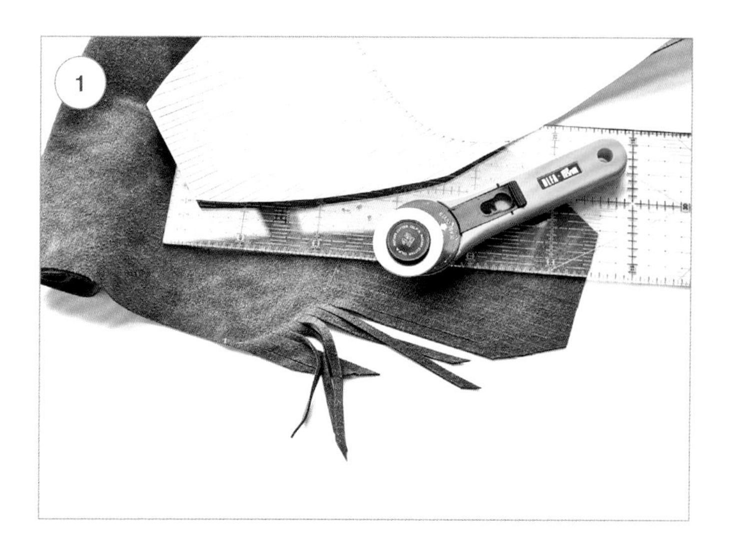

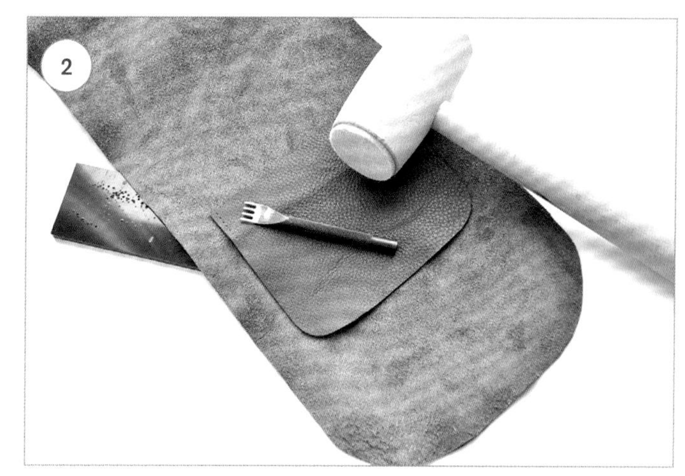

BEFORE YOU START

Cut out the pattern pieces on pages 64–5: 2 x front/back panel, flap, and pocket (optional). For the back and flap: if the size of the leather allows you to work in one piece, join the pattern pieces at the dots. Otherwise add a ⅜in (1cm) seam allowance to the top of the back panel and the flap. All other seam allowances are included on the pattern pieces.

Trace the pattern pieces onto the leather and cut out. From medium weight leather scraps, additionally cut two ¾ x 2in (2 x 5cm) strips for the tabs.

1 On the wrong side of the flap, mark the leather at approximately ¼in (5mm) intervals as shown on the template using a quilter's grid ruler if you have one to hand. Using a rotary cutter or scissors cut the fringe.

2 To make the inner pocket, trace the position of the pocket onto the wrong side of the back panel. Using double-sided removable tape secure the pocket in place on the wrong side of the back panel. Using a pricking iron and hammer or a stitching awl make sewing holes at regular intervals about ⅛–¼in (3mm–5mm) from the edge and through both layers of leather.

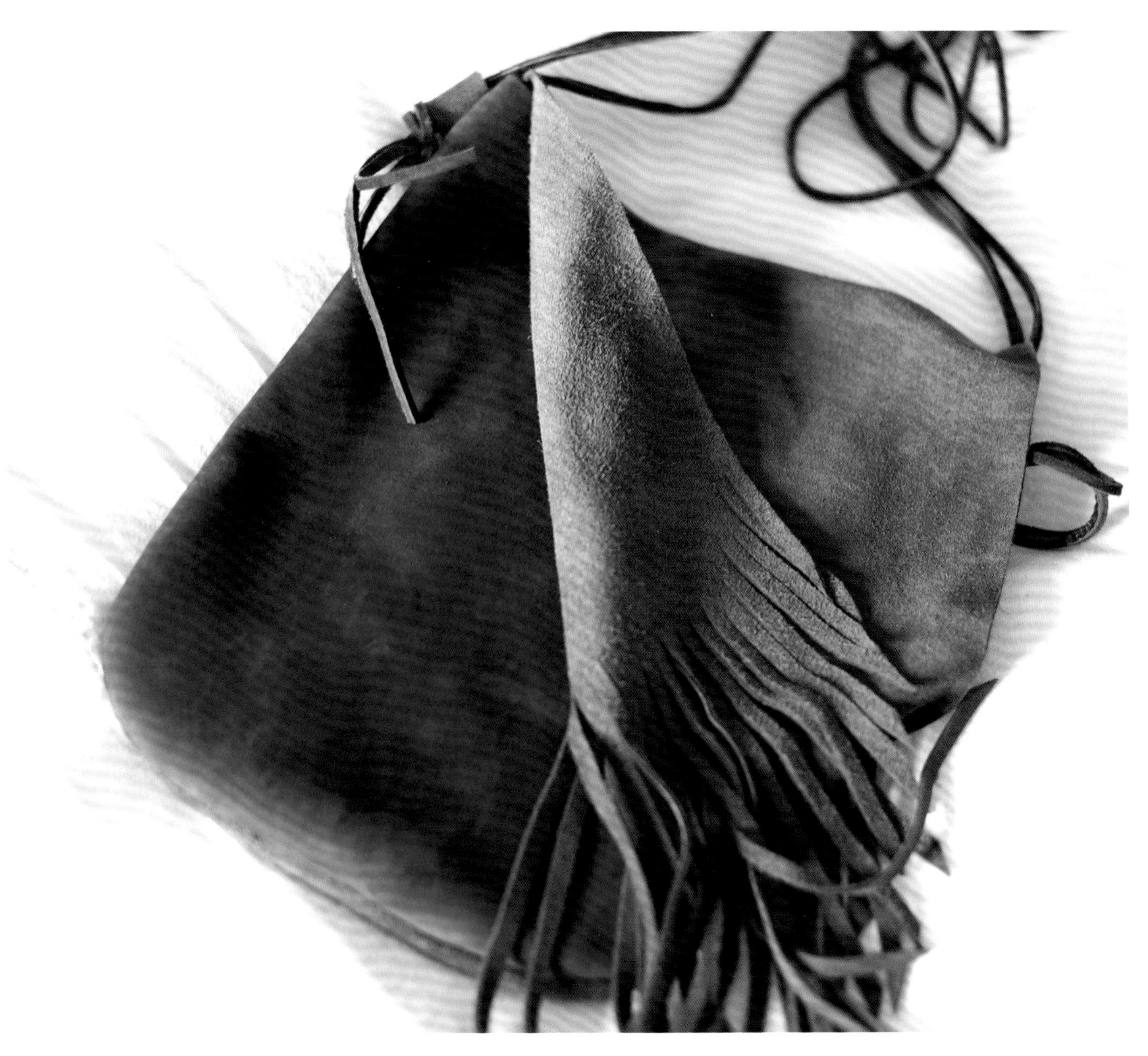

3 Sew into place using saddle stitch (see page 63). Make sure to use even tension as you sew, as the stitches will show at the back.

4 Make stitching holes for the side seam in front and back panels with a pricking iron or awl, about ⅛–¼in (3mm–6mm) from the edge. When using an awl, the size of the stitches should be no longer than ⅛in (3mm). When using two pieces of leather for the back panel and flap, make additional stitching holes along the top, about ¼in (6mm) from the top. Make stitching holes in the short sides of the two tab pieces as well.

5 Join the back panel and flap, if working with two pieces: place both pieces on top of each other by overlapping them at the stitch line, the right sides of both pieces facing up. Sew them together using saddle stitch – this will give you one long flat panel.

6 Join the front and back panel: place the front and back panel on top of each other, right sides facing, squeeze the tabs folded in half between both layers about ⅜in (1cm) from the top of the front panel, making sure all stitch lines coincide. Sew together using saddle stitch.

7 Turn the bag inside out and roll the seam between your fingers to set and shape the bag.

8 To make the strap, take the three strands of leather cording and tie them together with a big knot at one end. Pull the three strands through both tabs and finish off with another knot.

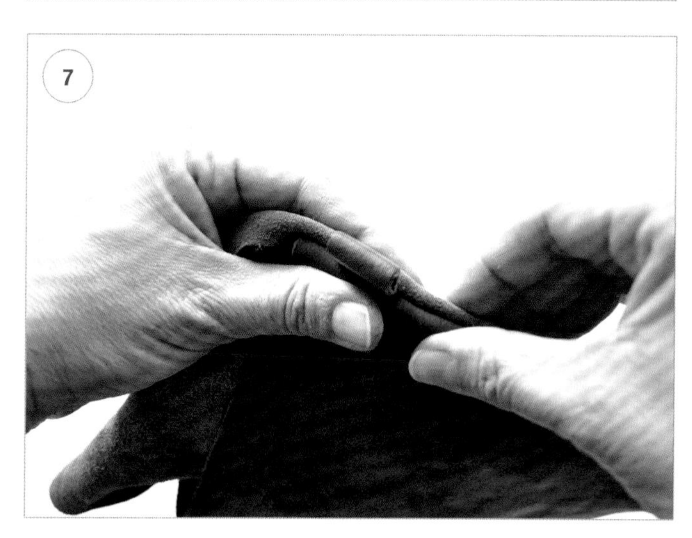

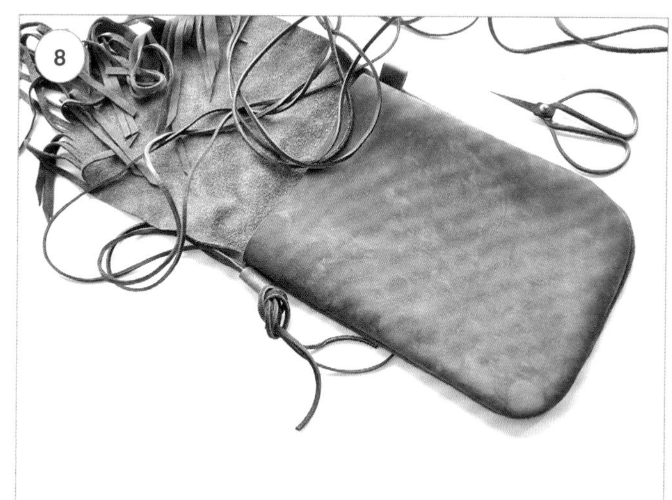

SADDLE STITCH

Slip a needle to both ends of a long strand of sewing thread. Lock the needles by piercing the thread two or three times with the needle and pulling the threaded needle through. Twist a couple of times. Next, push one needle through the first stitch hole and pull until the thread on either side of the work is of equal length. Make one or two overcast stitches through the first hole. Hold one needle in each hand. Push the first needle through the next hole, immediately followed by pushing the other needle through that same hole. Tug the thread on either side with equal tension to ensure nice, even stitches without pulling too hard. Repeat in the same way, alternating between needles, all the way down the seam. Finish by running back over a couple of stitches. Secure with a knot and cut.

Photocopy both pattern pieces at 139%
for actual size

TEMPLATES

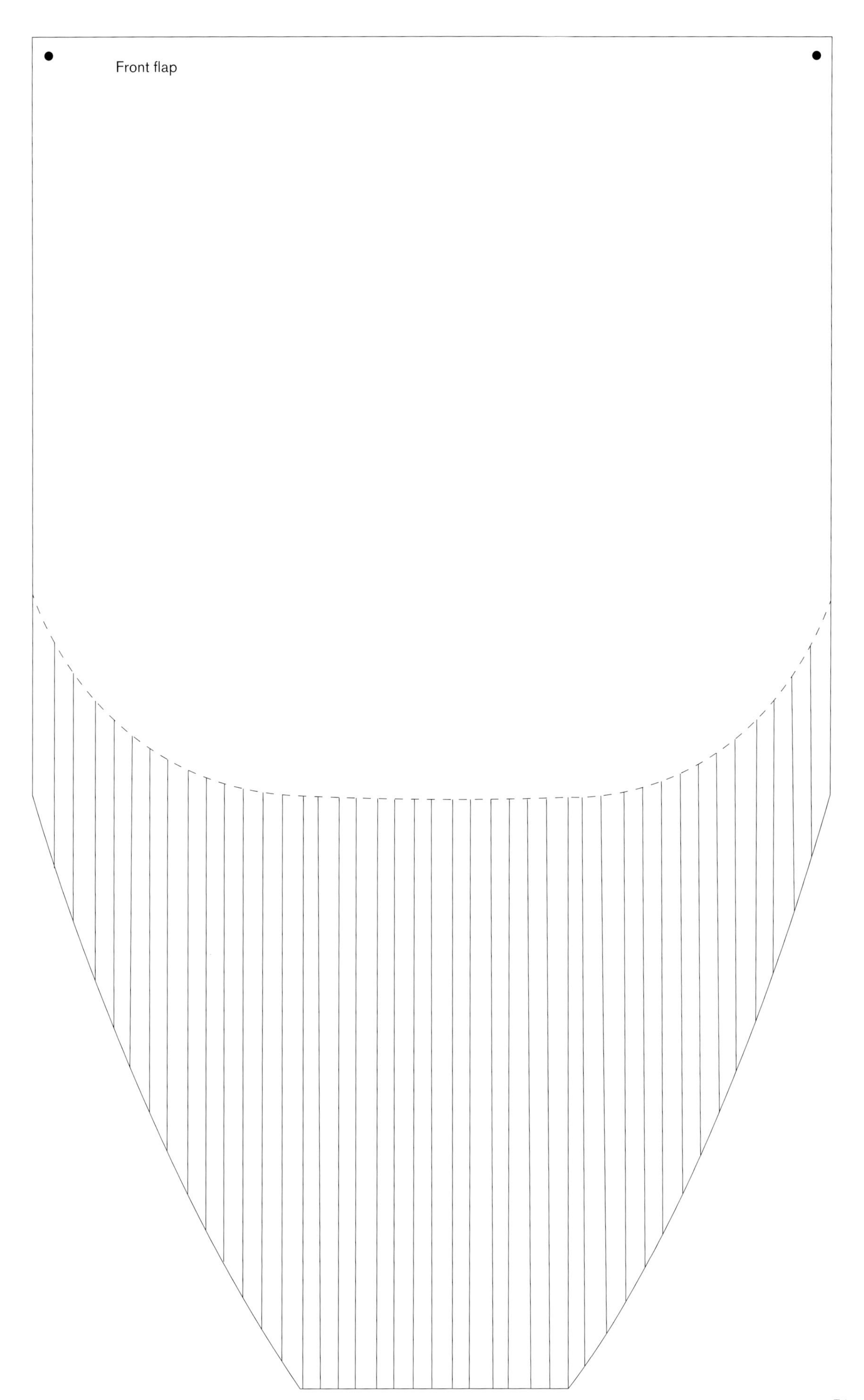
Front flap

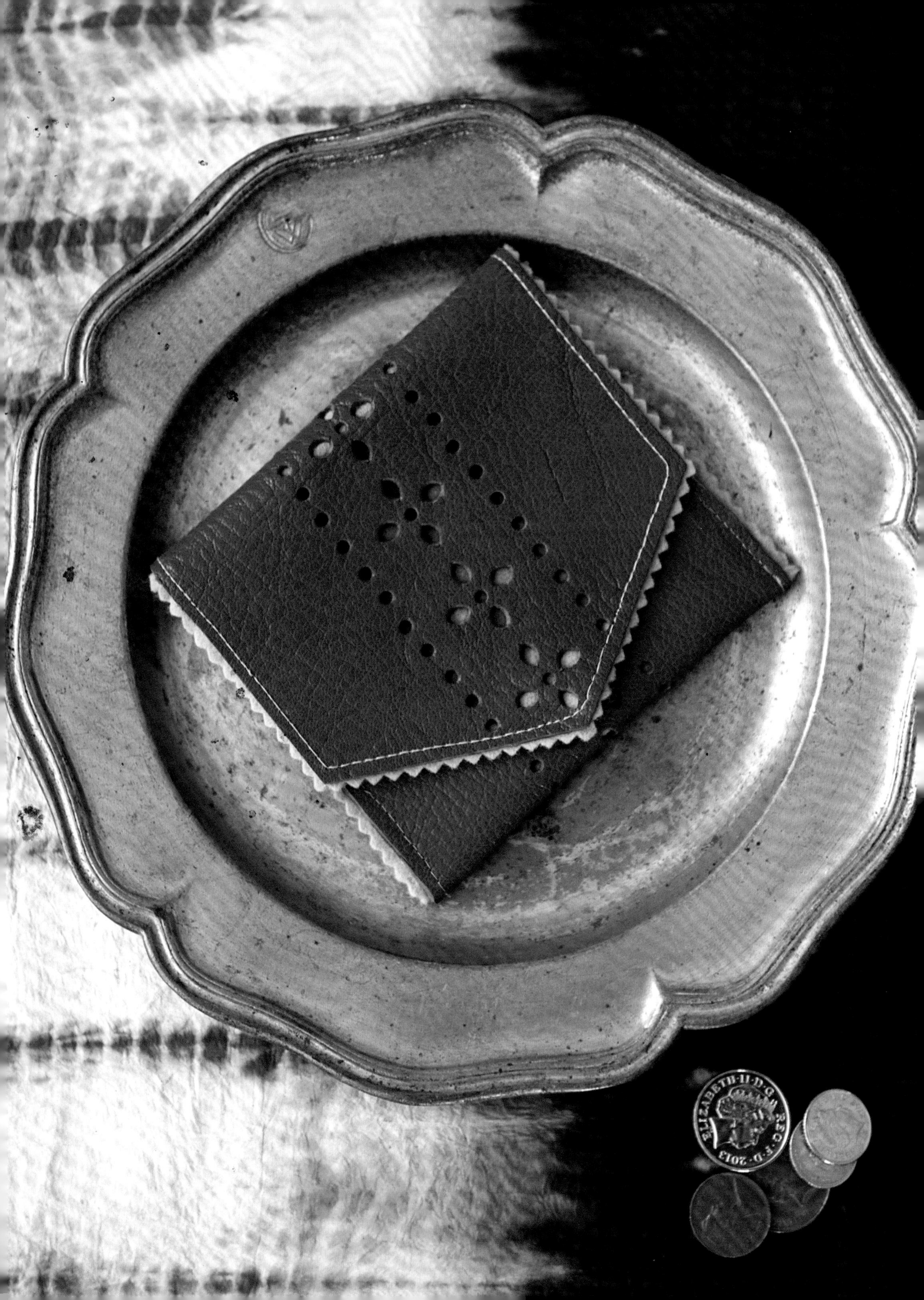
ELIZABETH·II·D·G·REG·F·D·2013

Punched leather purse

Make a simple leather purse in contrasting colours. Practise sewing with scraps through two thicknesses of both felt and leather before stitching your purse.

Materials

- 12½ x 5½in (32 x 14cm) piece of leather
- 12½ x 5½in (32 x 14cm) plus ¾in (2cm) square piece of felt
- 3mm hole punch
- 7mm curved lino cutter
- Magnetic snap fastener
- Sharp scissors
- Pinking shears
- Masking tape
- Steel ruler and scalpel (optional)
- Sewing machine
- Thread to match your felt colour
- Fabric glue
- Sewing needle

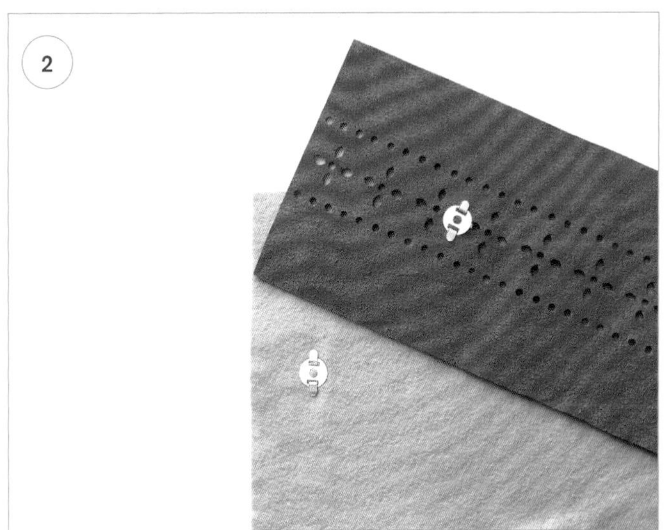

1 Photocopy or trace the template on page 69 and cut it out. Using small strips of masking tape, attach it to the right side of your strip of leather and firstly punch out the dots with a 3mm leather punch, then use two cuts with the lino tool to cut out the petal shapes. Use sharp scissors or a scalpel and steel ruler to cut the leather around the edge of the template.

2 Attach the two halves of the magnetic fastener to the leather approximately 3in (8cm) from the straight end, and the felt ¾in (2cm) from one end.

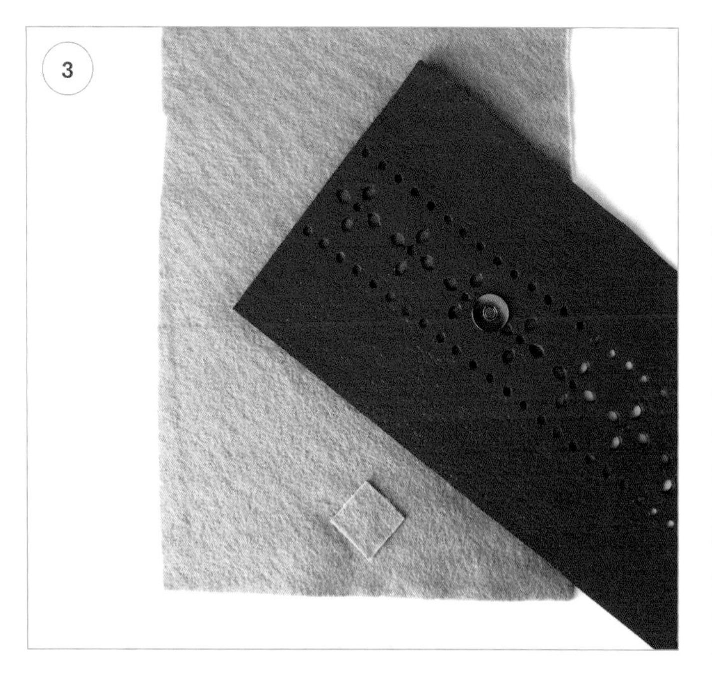

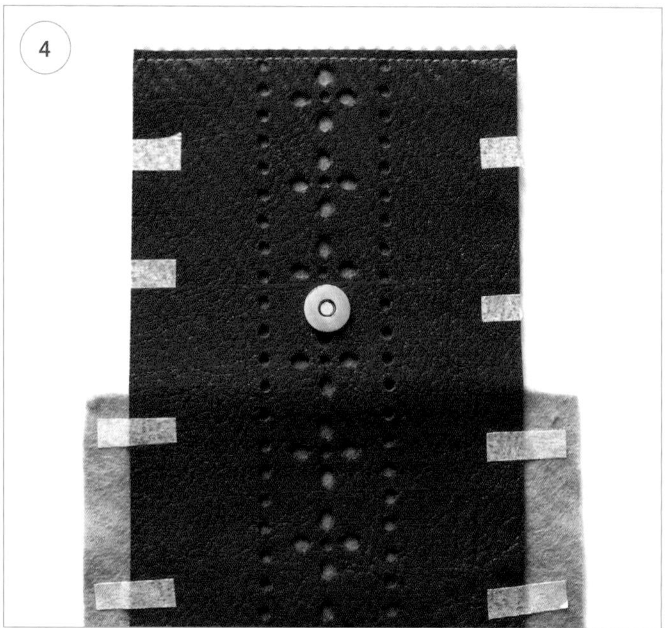

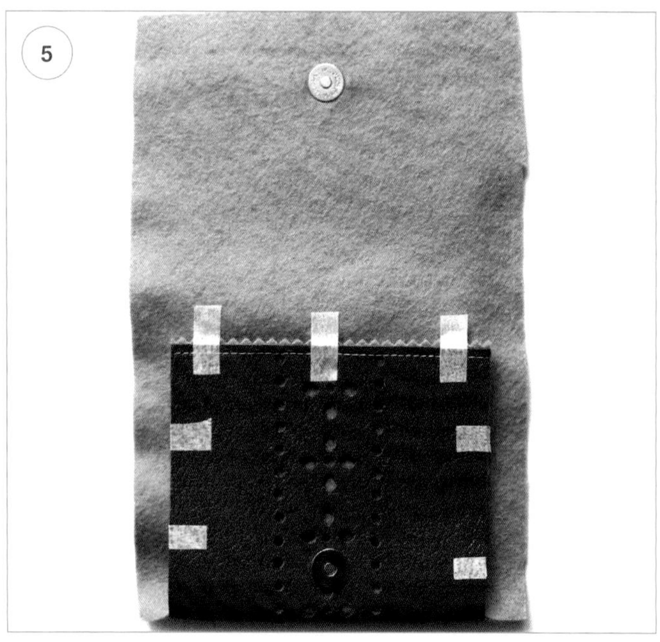

3 Use fabric glue to cover the back of the magnetic fastener with a ¾in (2cm) square of felt.

4 Attach the leather strip, right side down, centred on the felt, with small strips of masking tape. Stitch along the top edge, about ⅛in (3mm) from the edge of the leather. Finish the thread ends off using a needle. Trim the felt along the stitched edge using the pinking shears. With sharp scissors, cut the felt flush to the edge of the leather to a point about 4¼in (10.5cm) down each side from the stitched edge.

5 With the leather side down, fold the bottom section up 4¼in (10.5cm) and attach along the pinked edge using strips of masking tape. At this point, take care that you have folded accurately so that the front and back of the leather side edges align.

6 Turn the work over and carefully stitch through all four layers from one bottom (folded) corner, up to the point and down the other side, about ⅛in (3mm) from the edge of the leather. Finish off the ends by hand with a needle and finally trim all the felt with the pinking shears.

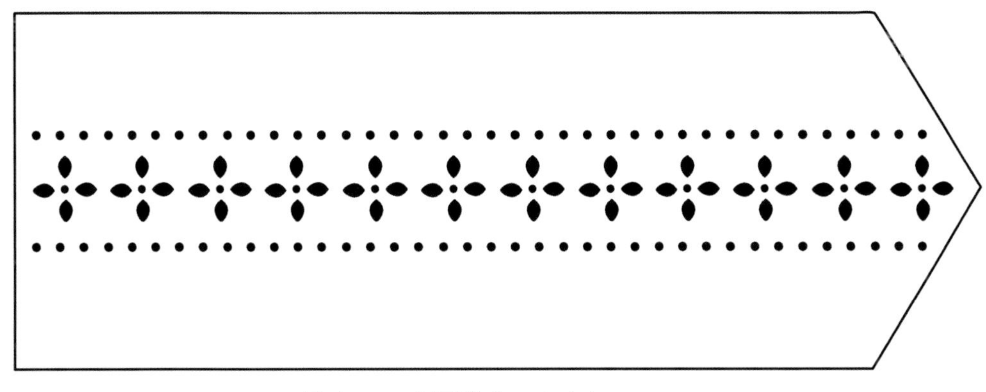

Photocopy at 250% for actual size

TEMPLATE

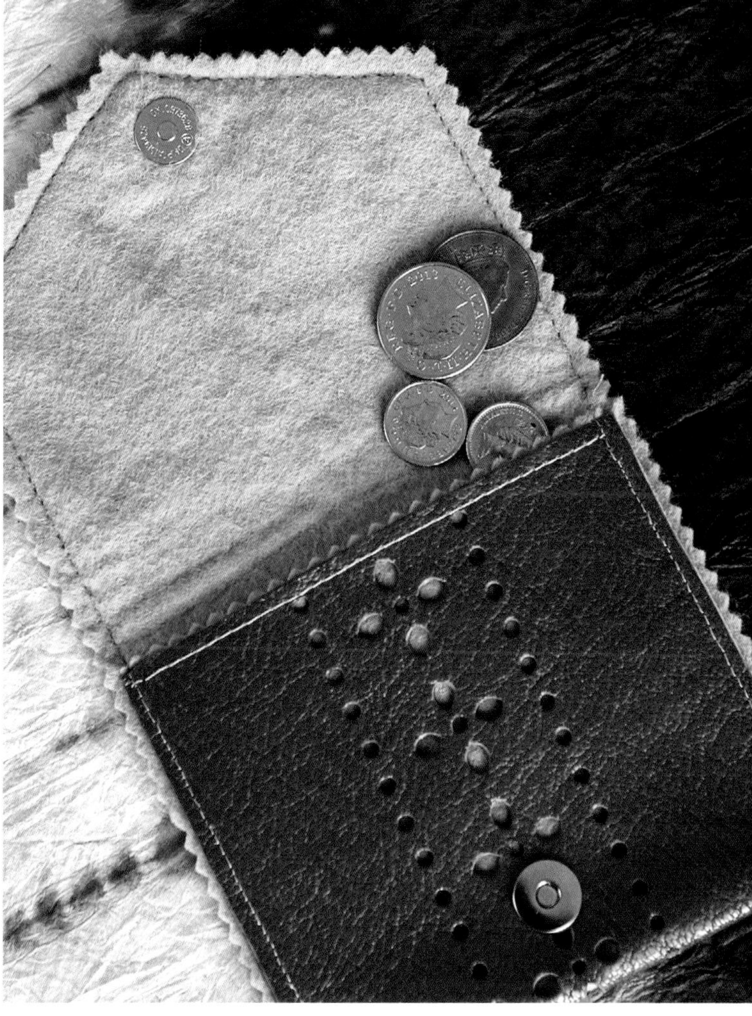

Clutch bag

See pretty friendship bracelets in a new light by using them to embellish beautiful soft leather. This bag could easily be adapted to make a tablet cover.

Materials

- 12 x 22in (30 x 55cm) soft leather
- Sewing thread to match your leather
- 2mm, 3mm and 4mm metal punches
- Hammer
- Scalpel or small sharp scissors
- Selection of cotton embroidery threads
- Safety pins (for making the friendship bracelets)
- 1 x medium Sam Browne stud
- Flat-head screwdriver
- 2mm (UK14:USB/1) crochet hook
- Sewing machine
- A4 sheet of tissue or tracing paper

Tip

Tie extra knots at either end of the bracelets after step 6 if you feel they are not securely anchored at the back of the leather.

1 Photocopy the template on page 73 to size, cut out the leather for your bag using sharp scissors. Use 2mm and 3mm metal punches as indicated on the template to make holes on the front of your bag. Cut a ⅜in (1cm) slit from the centre of the punched hole (A) away from the edge of the flap as indicated on the pattern using small sharp scissors or a scalpel.

2 Fold the leather with smooth sides facing, so that the dots indicated on the pattern align. Tear your tissue or tracing paper into four equal strips along its length. Sandwich each side seam between two strips of paper and stitch them about ⅛in (3mm) in from the edge, reverse stitching at the top edge for extra strength.

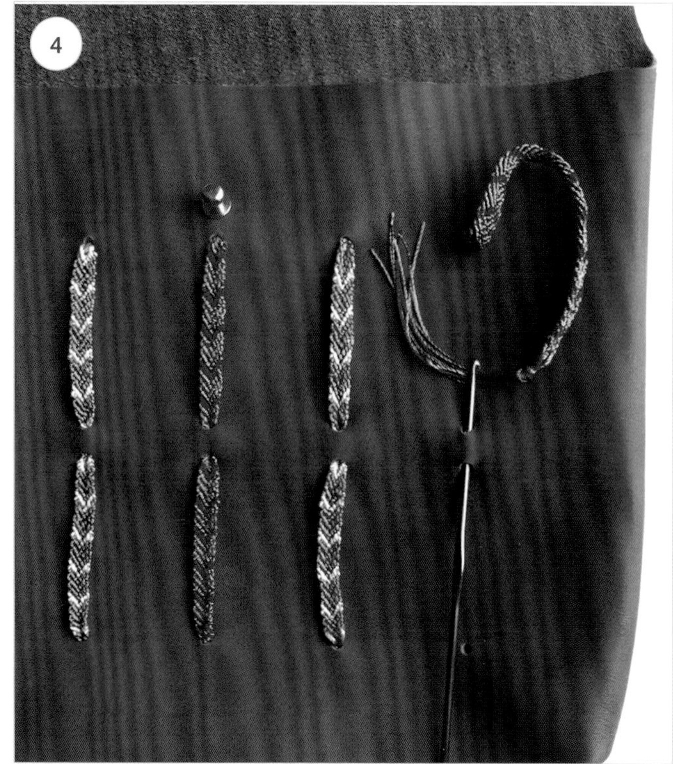

3 With your bag still inside out, flatten the two bottom corners and stitch across the two triangular corners about 1⅜in (3.5cm) from the points at a 45-degree angle to create a flat bottom to your bag.

4 Fix the Sam Browne stud in place at the top front of the bag, tightening it with a screwdriver.

5 Make five friendship bracelets, each one about 5in (12cm) long, using various colour combinations of the embroidery threads (a good online tutorial for making friendship bracelets can be found at friendship-bracelets.net/tutorials.php).

6 Inset a 2mm crochet hook through from the back of one of the top holes along the front face of your bag to the front. Hook the loop at the top of one of your friendship bracelets and pull it through to the back of the leather, giving it a final firm tug to pass the knot through the hole. Use the hook to pull the bracelet through to the back of the bag through the next hole down, then out again through the next one to the front of the bag. Finally, hook the thread ends and knot through the bottom hole. Trim the end of the threads to about ¾in (2cm).

7 Repeat step 6 with the remaining four bracelets (image 4).

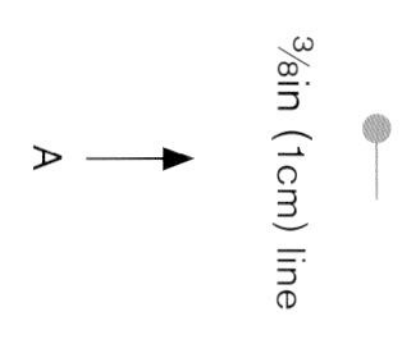

Includes ⅜in (1cm) seam allowance
Cut 1

TEMPLATE

Printed at approximately 25% of
actual size, but can be reproduced
to the size you wish

Green dots = 2mm holes
Purple dots = 3mm holes

Coin purse

Keep your change in this simple coin purse. You can make it right-handed (with the fold on the right side) or left-handed (with the fold on the left) simply by flipping the template before cutting the leather.

Materials

- $8\frac{1}{2}$ x $8\frac{1}{2}$in (22 x 22cm) piece of medium- to heavyweight leather
- 2 snap buttons, $\frac{5}{8}$in (15mm) in diameter
- Snap button pliers or other snap setting tool (often provided with the snaps)
- Leather punch or any other piercing tool
- Pricking iron or stitching awl
- Wooden or rubber mallet to use with pricking iron
- 2 heavy-duty sewing needles
- Heavy-duty thread (waxed linen or nylon)
- Rotary cutter or craft knife
- Cutting mat
- Glue
- Scissors
- Pen
- Ruler
- Round corner leather punch (optional)

The dimensions of the finished product are approximately $4\frac{1}{4}$ x 4in (10.5 x 10cm)

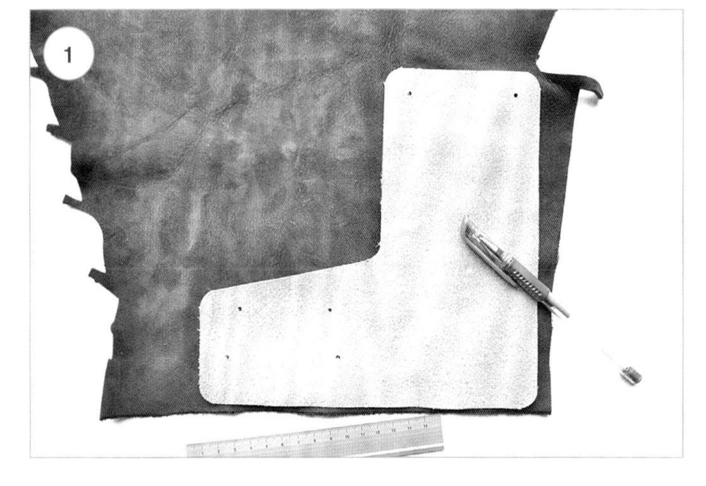

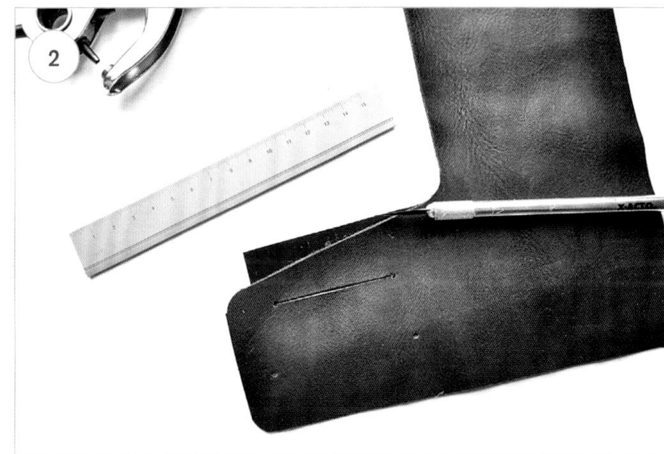

1 Copy and cut out the template on page 77. Make holes in the template for the positioning of the snap buttons and the card slot as indicated. Trace the template onto the wrong side of the leather. Copy the positioning of the snap buttons and card slot onto the piece of leather.

2 Using a leather punch, make the holes for snap buttons and card slot as indicated. Finish making the card slot, connecting the two holes as indicated on the template, using a craft knife or a rotary cutter.

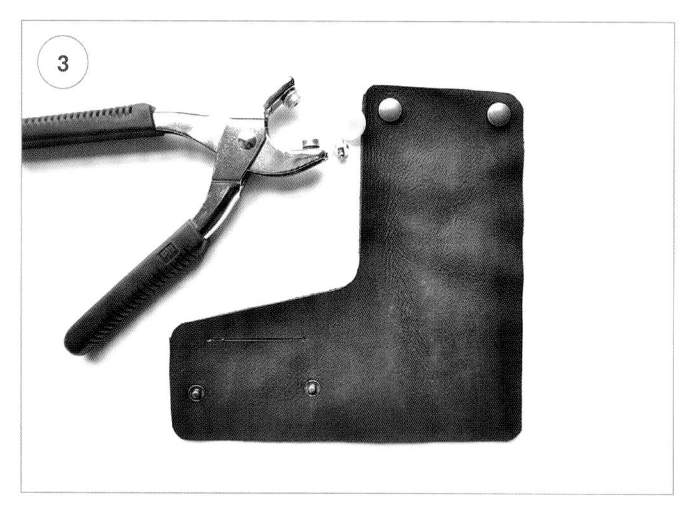
3

4

5

6

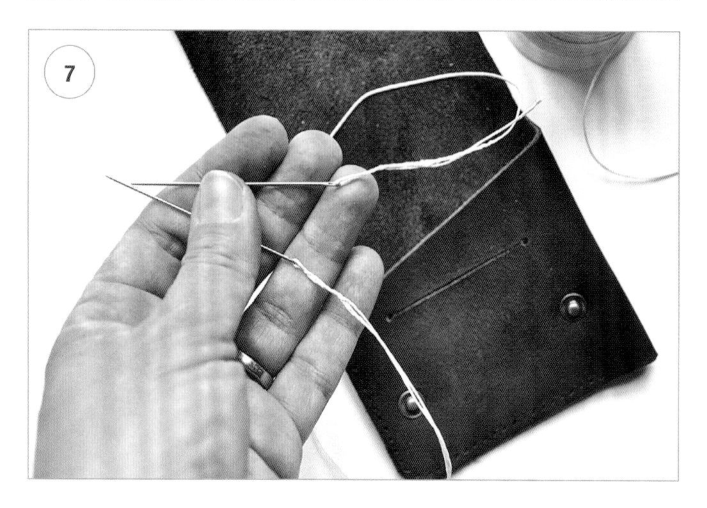
7

8

3 Set the snaps as shown.

4 To align the edges perfectly and hold them in place for sewing, apply a small amount of glue along the sewing line and fold the leather in place making sure the edges line up. Note how the sewing line doesn't go all the way down to the corners. Leave to dry for at least 10 minutes.

5 Once the glue has dried, it's time to make the sewing holes with a stitching iron or awl.

6 Cut a piece of thread of approximately 24in (60cm) long, or roughly five times the length of the seam, and thread a needle at each end.

7 Lock the needles by piercing the thread two to three times with the needle and pulling the thread all the way through. Twist a couple of times.

8 Next, push one needle through the first stitch hole and pull until the thread on either side is of equal length. Make one or two overcast stitches through the first hole. Hold one needle in each hand. Push the first needle through the next hole, immediately followed by pushing the other needle through that same hole. Tug the thread on either side with equal tension to ensure nice, even stitches without pulling too hard.

9 Repeat in the same way, alternating between needles, all the way down the seam. Finish with a few overcast stitches and by running back over a couple of stitches. Then cut the thread.

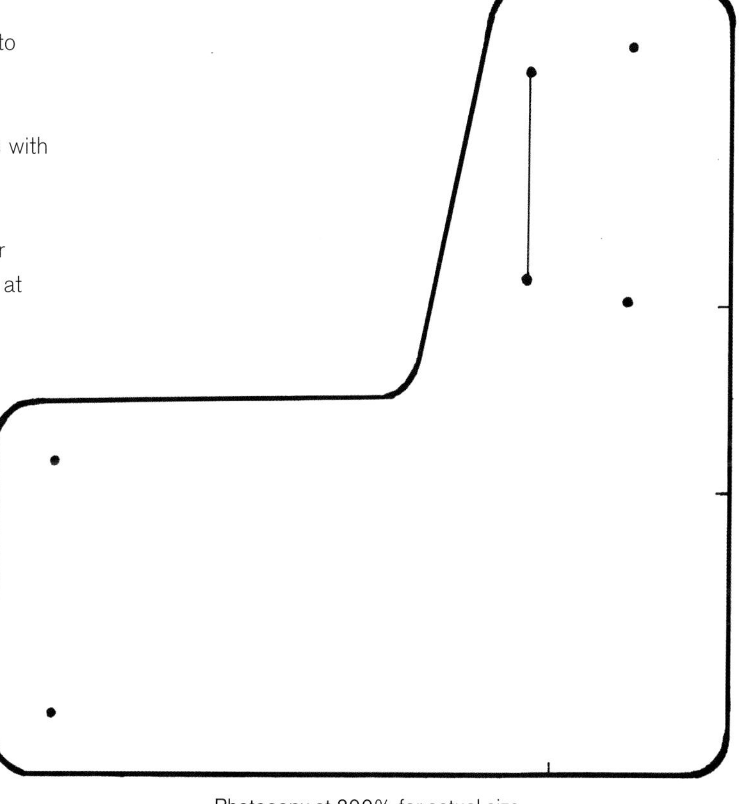

Photocopy at 200% for actual size

TEMPLATE

Studded tote

Put your own stamp on the classic tote
by using faux leather and studded detailing.

Materials

- Faux leather cut to size: 1 x main piece, 43 x 14½in (110 x 37cm); 2 x side panels, 18½ x 6in (47cm x 15cm); 2 x handles, 35 x 4in (89 x 10cm)
- Quilting thread (strong sewing thread)
- Sewing needle
- Scissors
- Ruler
- White pen
- Stud kit
- ½in (12mm) eyelet kit
- Embroidery cotton and needle
- Sewing machine
- Hammer

1 Take the largest piece of faux leather and use a ruler to measure the centre point and mark it with a white pen. This is the centre point for your stud and eyelet pattern. Use a ruler and a white pen to mark dots for positioning your eyelets and studs.

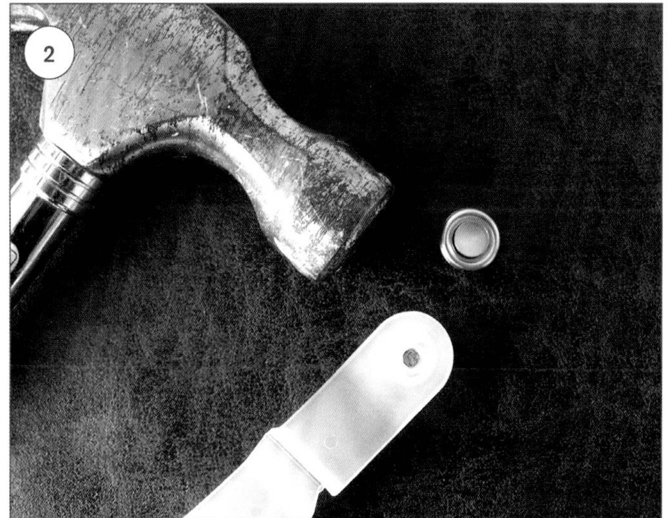

2 Either follow the template on page 81, or lay the studs and eyelets out on a large sheet of paper to create your own pattern. You will have to cut the plastic jig for the eyelets in half where it folds in order to use it, as when in one piece it only allows you to fix eyelets within a few centimetres of the edge of your fabric. The studs and eyelets will come with instructions. Follow the instructions on the kit, taking time to position one half of the jig underneath the fabric and the other on top before whacking it with your hammer to finish. Repeat steps 1 and 2 at the other end of the piece of faux leather.

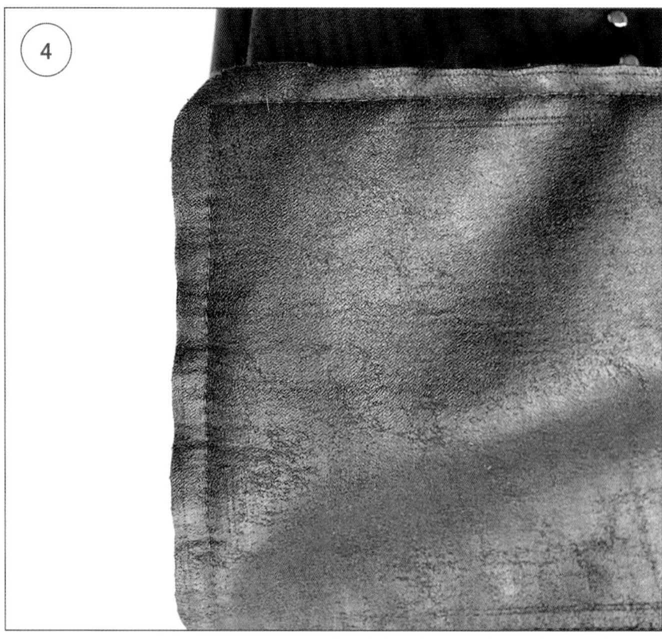

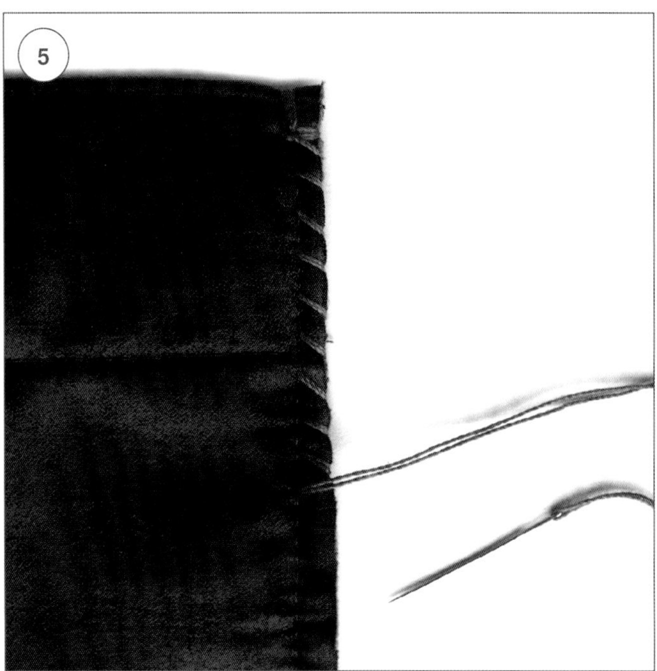

3 Set your sewing machine to a large stitch and thread up with quilting thread. Fold both short ends over 2in (5cm) to the wrong side and stitch down by machine about ⅛in (3mm) from the raw edge. Do the same with one end of each of the side panels. The nature of faux leather means that it can stick to the bed of your machine, so encourage it along under the foot as you work.

4 Join one side panel to the main piece. Place one side of the top hemmed edge of one side panel to the right hand top edge of one hemmed end of the main piece, right sides together. Machine a ¼in (6mm) seam down to the first corner of the side panel. Leaving the machine needle down in the fabric, raise the foot and swivel and manipulate your two layers of fabric to turn the corner. Continue stitching, repeating the corner turn at the next corner of the panel and finish stitching the seam up to the top hemmed edges. Finish off all the thread ends by hand. At this point you can trim the corners at the bottom of the panel slightly to reduce bulk. Repeat with the other side of the bag.

5 Use the embroidery thread doubled to 'whip' the side seams with overstitch, making two or three stitches on top of one another at the top edges for extra strength Take one handle piece and fold it into thirds so that it measures just over 1¼in (3cm) wide. Machine stitch around all sides a few millimetres in from the edges. Position one end of the handle on the inside of the top opening of the bag on the main piece and 3½in (9cm) from the stitched side seam. Align its bottom edge with the stitched hem. Machine it in position and finish off all the thread ends by hand. Repeat with the other end of the handle 3½in (9cm) from the other side seam. Repeat with the second handle.

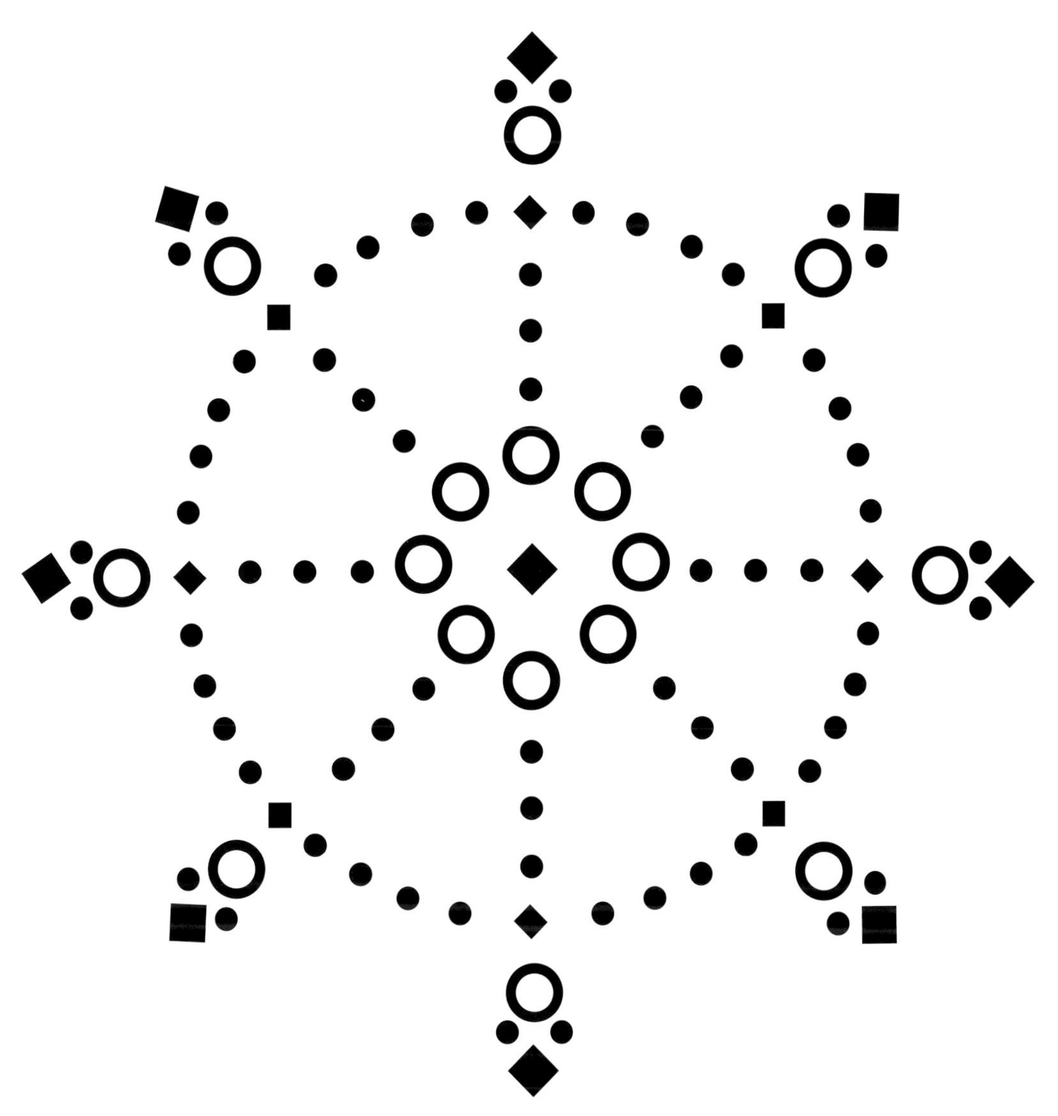

Photocopy at 200% for actual size

TEMPLATE

Academy Watercolour
DERWENT
Academy Watercolour

For the home

Blue
Academy Watercolour
DERWENT
Academy Watercolour
Academy Watercolour

Pencil cases

Make a clever and versatile pencil case from scrap leather in two simple designs.

Pencil case with snap buttons

Materials

- 7 x 10½in (18cm x 26cm) piece of medium- to heavyweight leather
- 4 snap buttons, ⅝in (15mm) in diameter
- Leather punch or any other piercing tool
- Snap button pliers or other snap setting tool (often provided with the snaps)
- Rotary cutter
- Scissors
- Pen
- Ruler
- Cutting mat

Tip

If you only have lightweight leather to hand, you can line the leather by ironing some fabric to the back, using double-sided fabric adhesive to bond the pieces together.

1 Photocopy the template on page 86 then cut out and make holes as indicated for the positioning of the snaps. Trace the template on the wrong side of the leather and mark the positioning of the snaps on the leather.

2 Cut out the leather using rotary cutters. Trim the rounded corners with scissors.

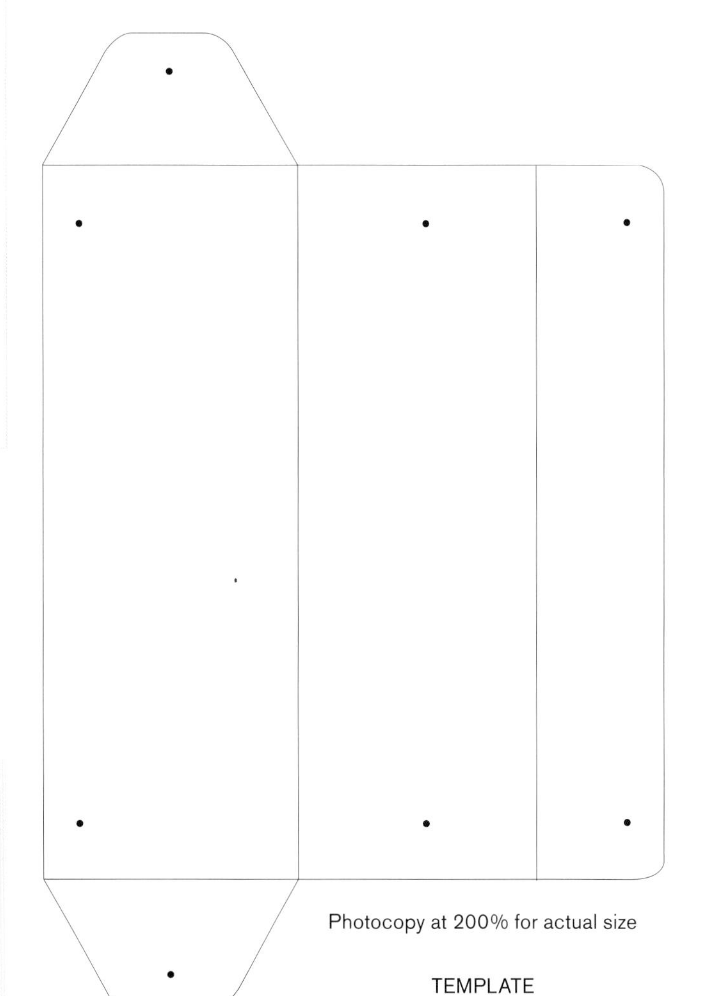

Photocopy at 200% for actual size

TEMPLATE

3 With a leather punch or any other piercing tool, make the holes for the snaps.

4 Set the snaps in place using snap button pliers or any other snap setting tool (images 4 and 5). Close the snaps and fix the creases by gently rubbing the leather with your fingers.

Tips

Alter the template to fit bigger pens, more or fewer pens, or to include an eraser or pencil sharpener. This design could also be used to hold your make-up brushes.

Cutting through leather tends to dull the blade of a rotary cutter. Keep a separate blade for projects involving leather.

Pencil case with elastic

Materials

- 8 x 11in (20 x 29cm) piece of medium- to heavyweight leather
- 20in (50cm) of ¼in (6mm) wide elastic
- 4 small double cap rivets for leather (optional)
- Rotary cutter
- Craft knife or scalpel
- Scissors
- Leather punch
- Big sewing needle or small safety pin
- Rivet setting tool or pliers (optional)
- Masking tape
- Ruler
- Pencil
- Cutting mat
- Clear nail polish or glue

1

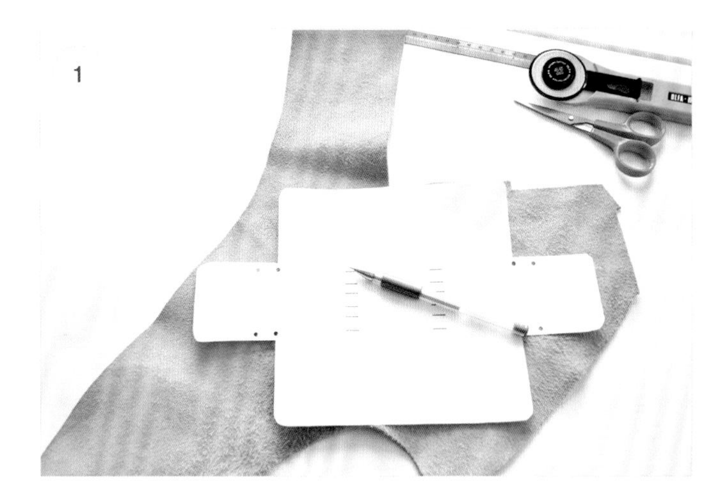

2

3

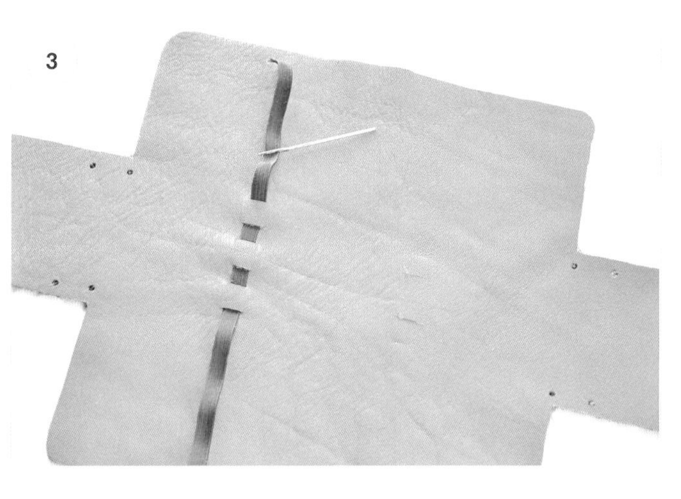

1 Photocopy and cut out the template on page 88. If planning on using rivets, make holes in the paper template as indicated. Trace the template onto the wrong side of the leather. With a pen, mark where the rivet holes should sit. Cut with a rotary cutter. Trim and round the corners with small scissors.

2 Use masking tape to mark out the cutting area. Copy the positioning for the horizontal incisions onto the masking tape as indicated on the template. Start cutting through the leather with a craft knife or scalpel, making sure only to cut the area between the masking tape, using the marks on the masking tape as a guide.

3 With a sewing needle or safety pin, thread the elastic through the incisions. Repeat for the second set of incisions. Before tying a knot, insert some pens and close the flaps to determine the exact length of the elastic. Keep in mind you want the elastic to snugly fit around the case. Cut off any excess elastic. Dab the ends with clear nail polish or glue to avoid fraying.

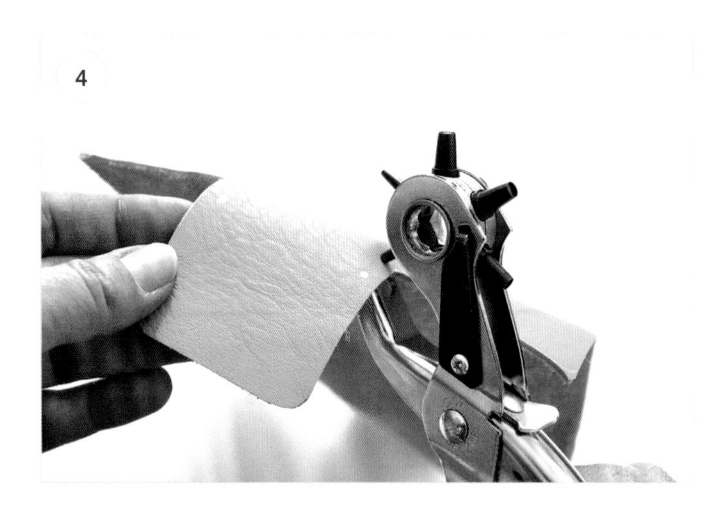

4 Optional: you can keep the flaps in place with rivets. Prepare the leather by making the holes for the rivets with a leather punch.

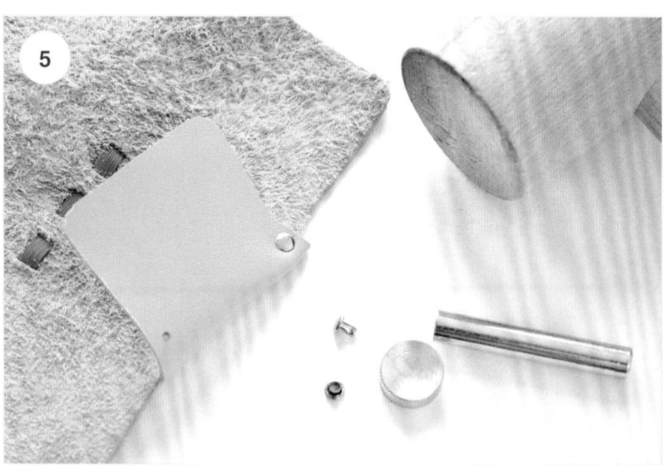

5 Set the rivets with a rivet setting tool or with rivet setting pliers.

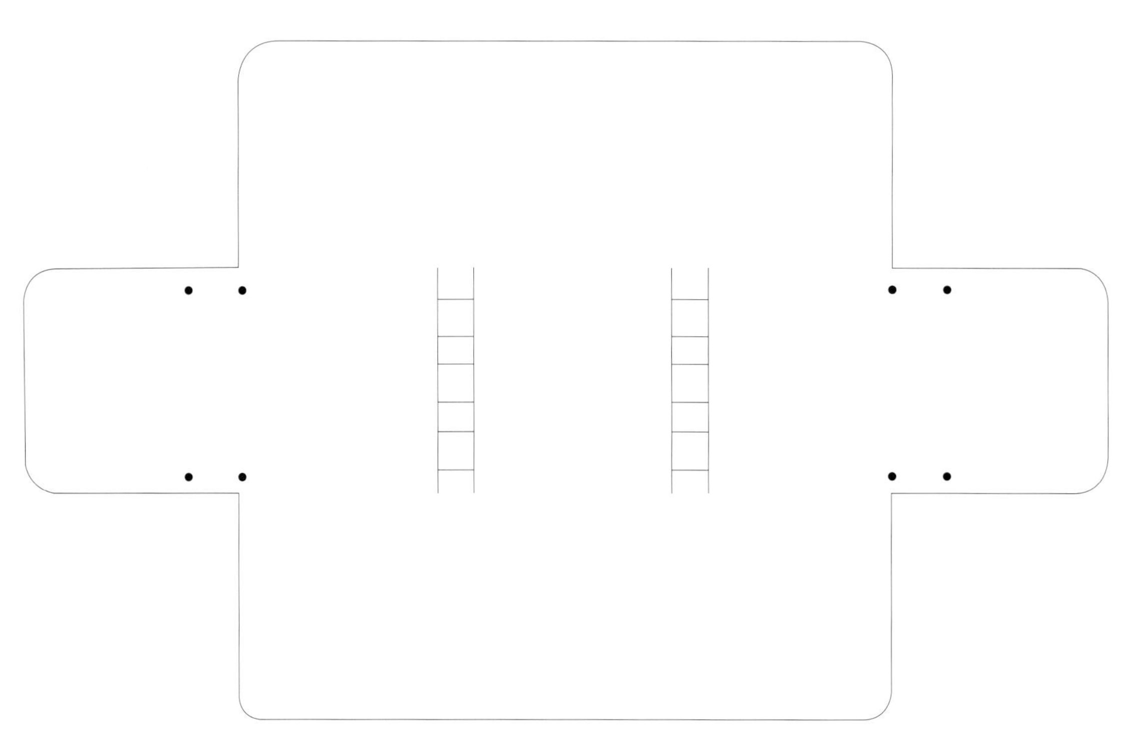

Photocopy at 200% for actual size

TEMPLATE

Academy Watercolour
Academy Watercolour

Booklets

Make beautiful leather notebooks in next to no time and keep them handy for travelling, doodling, or to give as a present.

Materials

For a 4¼ x 6in (10.5 x 15cm) notebook:

- Medium- to heavyweight leather: 9 x 6¼in (23 x 16cm) for simple booklet, 10½ x 6¼in (27 x 16cm) for booklet with flap
- 10–15 A5 sheets of paper
- 35in (90cm) leather shoelace
- Linen thread
- Embroidery needle
- Rotary cutter and cutting mat
- Leather punch and/or stitching awl
- Round corner punch (optional)
- Leather alphabet stamps (optional)
- Ruler
- Pen
- White glue (optional)

Tips

You can further personalize the notebook using leather alphabet stamps, paint or beads.

You can attach an end of leather shoelace at the top of the spine as a book mark.

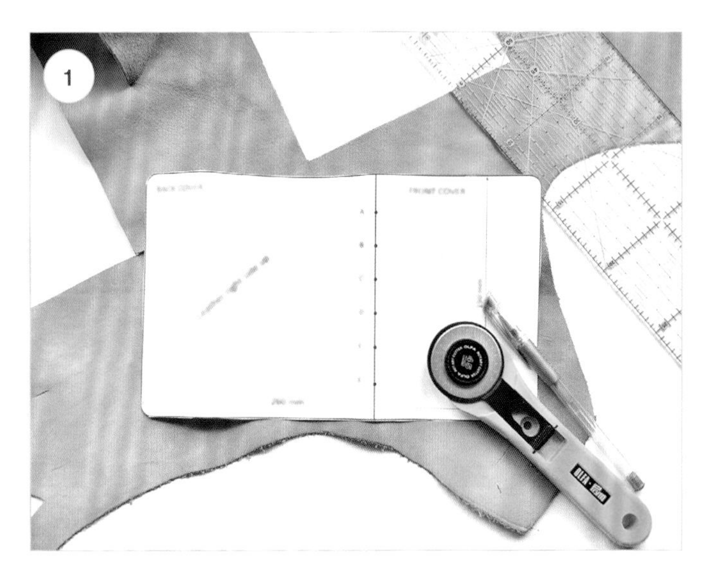

1 Photocopy and cut out the template for the simple leather book cover or the book cover with flap on page 93. Copy the positioning of the stitch holes (spine) and closure and make holes in the template accordingly.

2 Transfer the template onto a piece of leather, making sure to copy the positioning of the stitch holes and closure holes. Cut the leather using a rotary cutter. Cut corners with a round corner punch (optional).

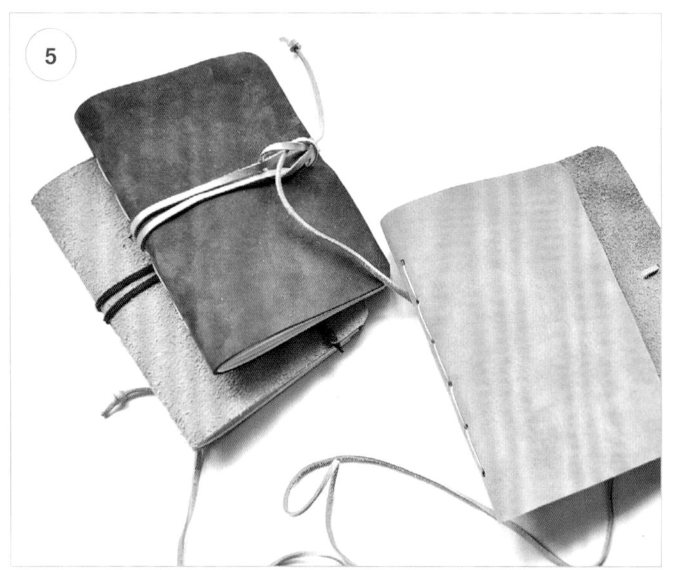

3 Fold the paper sheets in half. Transfer the position of the stitch holes onto one of the sheets to use as a template. Make holes with an awl correspondingly, doing this a few pages at a time. When done, arrange all the sheets to form a booklet.

4 Thread a needle with linen thread and tie a knot at the end. Place the leather cover on top of the paper arranged into a booklet. Using the template as a guide, sew the leather and paper together, going from A to B, to C, etc. When at F, sew your way back up to A and tie a knot. Cut off loose ends. Dab with a tiny amount of glue if you like, and leave to dry before closing the notebook.

5 Take the leather shoelace and thread it through the two holes on the front. Tie a knot at each end. Wrap the shoelace around the booklet and tie in a loose knot.

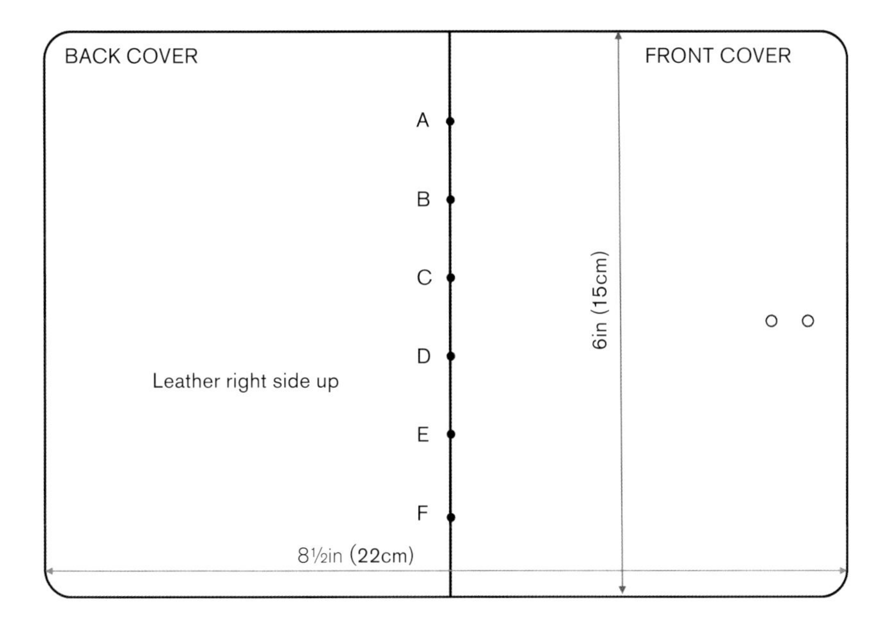

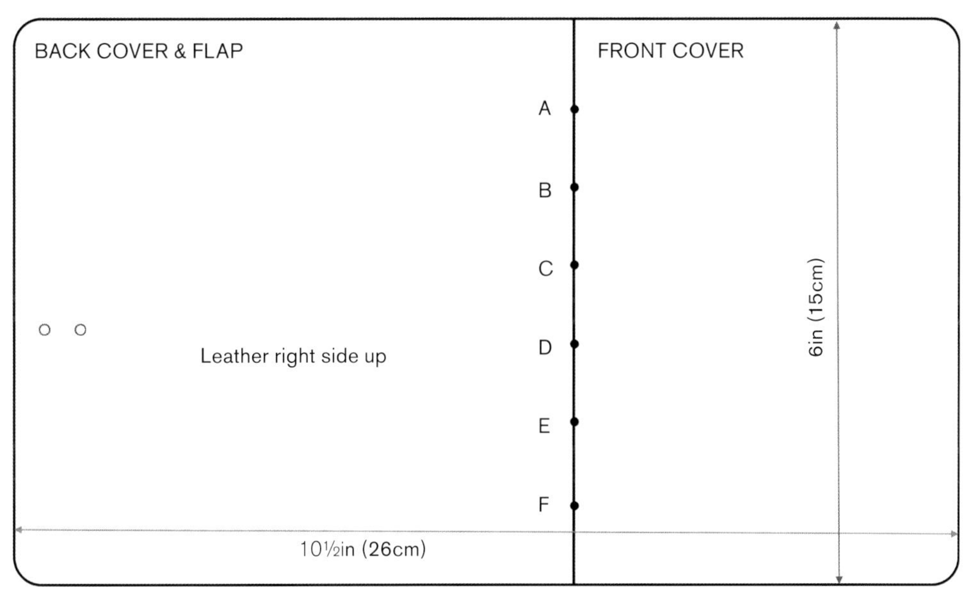

Photocopy at 200% for actual size

TEMPLATES

THE TWO BAYS

Writing set

Revive the gentle art of writing with this smart leather case. Incredibly stylish, it makes a practical companion for when you have to leave your desk, having a holder for a pen or pencil and handy stationery compartments.

Materials

- 18 x 18in (45 x 45cm) piece of leather
- Steel ruler, scalpel and cutting mat
- Masking tape
- 9 x 4¾in (23 x 12cm) piece of fabric
- 9in (23cm) diameter plate
- Pen
- Iron
- Quilting thread
- Sewing machine
- Leather sewing machine needle
- Scissors
- Sewing needle
- 7½ x 7in (19 x 18cm) piece of craft board
- Tissue paper
- Masking tape

BEFORE YOU START

Leather

Cut the leather into the following pieces using a scalpel and a steel ruler:

2 x inside lining pieces, 8¼ x 6in (21 x 15cm)
2 x pocket pieces, 8¼ x 4in (21 x 10cm)
1 x main piece, 9 x 18in (23 x 45cm)
1 x pen channel piece, 2½ x 4¾in (6 x 12cm)
1 x flap piece, 8¼ x 2½in (21 x 6cm)

Craft board

Cut the craft board into the following pieces using a scalpel and a steel ruler:

1 piece, 7½ x 1¾in (19 x 4.5cm)
2 pieces, 7½ x 5½in (19 x 13.5cm)

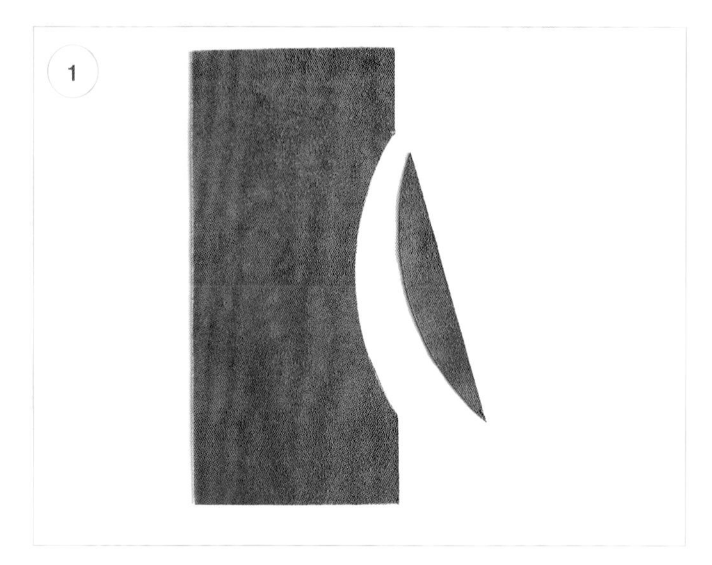

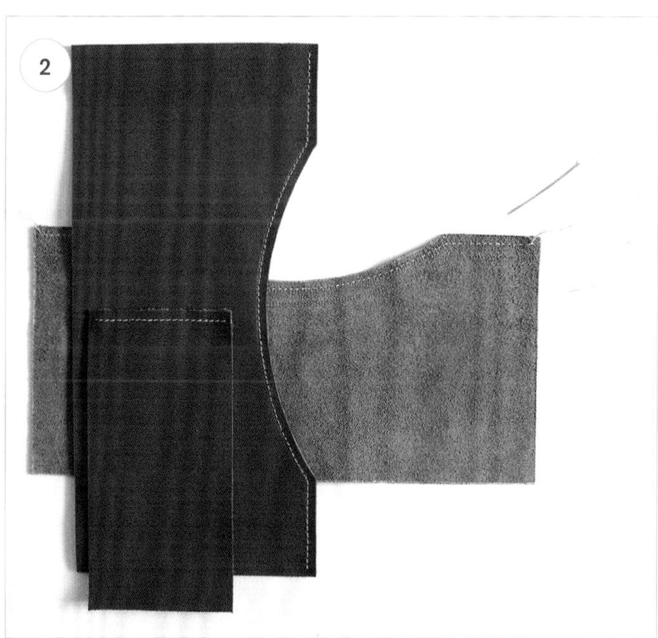

1 Take the two pocket pieces and draw a curve along one long edge of each using the curved edge of a plate, starting the curve roughly 1½in (4cm) from either end. Cut along the curve.

2 Machine stitch along the top of these two edges and one short end of the pen channel piece, about ⅛in (3mm) from the edge.

3 Fix one side of the magnetic snap, following the manufacturer's instructions, to the right side of the large leather piece centred on one short edge, 3in (7.5cm) in. Fix the other half to the leather flap piece, centred on the long edge and ¾in (2cm) in. Lay the large piece of leather face down. Use a pen to draw a ⅜in (1cm) border around all four edges. Take each of the strips of fabric and fold both short ends to the back ⅜in (1cm) and press with an iron. Position one 2in (5cm) from the left hand drawn line and one 1¼in (3cm) from the right hand drawn line.

4 Next, lay the pencil channel piece, right side up, to align with the bottom of the right hand fabric strip. Lay down the lining pieces right side up, then the flap and the pockets.

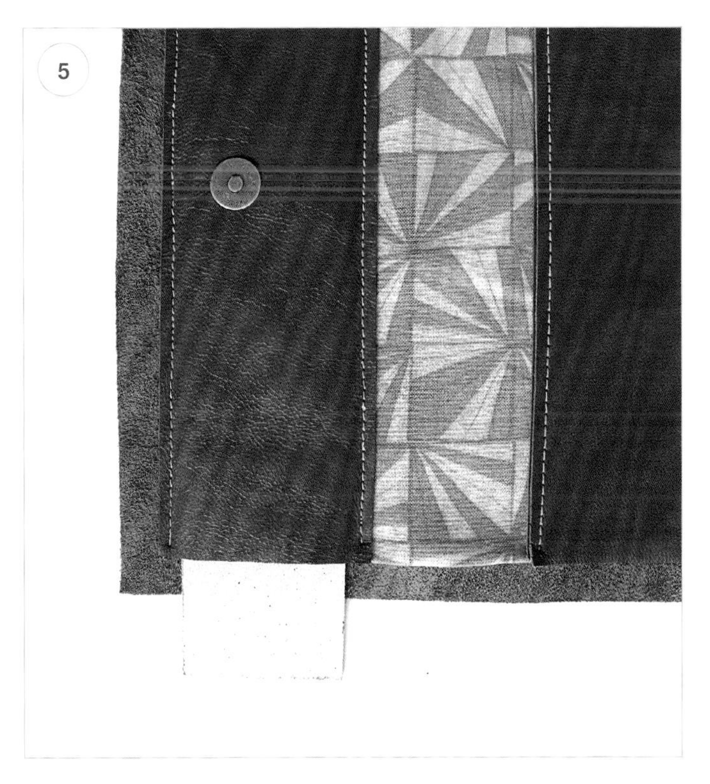

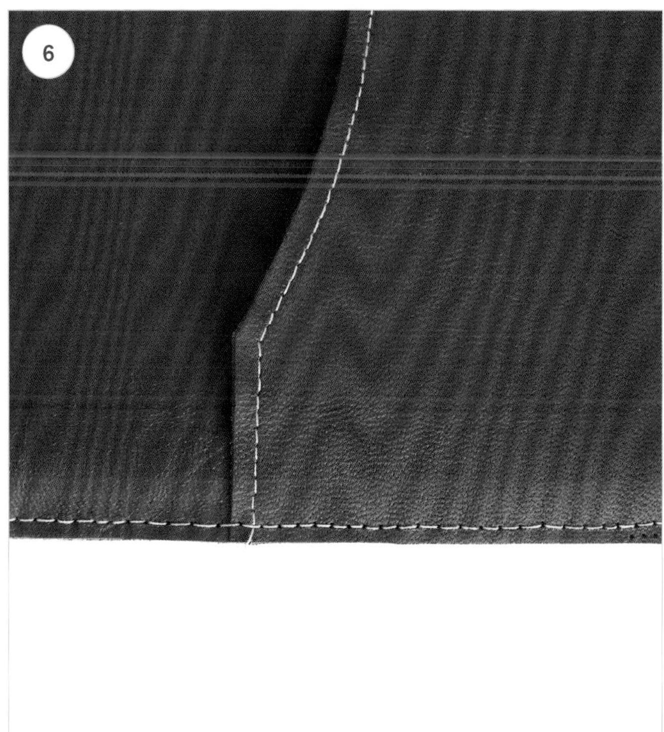

5 Secure all the pieces in position using small strips of masking tape. Machine stitch along the top roughly ⅛in (3mm) in from the edges. Stitch along all vertical seams: both sides of the flap, left-hand side of the left-hand pocket, right-hand side of the left-hand lining, left-hand side of the right-hand lining and finally along the right-hand edge. This will leave three open 'pockets' along the bottom edge for you to insert the card pieces.

6 Stitch along the bottom edge and trim off the excess of the large piece all around with sharp scissors.

Tip

Leather can stick to the sewing machine bed and make stitching awkward: sandwich the layers of leather between pieces of tissue paper to help your work. This will make it glide smoothly under the sewing foot while stitching. Tear the paper off after sewing – you may have to pick small bits out from underneath the stitching. Do so with a pin, taking care not to scratch the leather during the process.

iPad cover

The leather used for this elegant iPad cover is lined with a contrasting fabric, which makes the cut-out pattern stand out even more.

Materials

- 12 x 10in (30 x 25cm) medium weight vegetable tanned natural leather, for the front
- 12 x 10in (30 x 25cm) nubuck or another type of medium- to heavyweight leather, in a contrasting colour for the back
- 2 x 12 x 10in (30 x 25cm) cotton muslin, in a contrasting colour
- 2 x 12 x 10in (30 x 25cm) iron-on fabric adhesive papers
- Leather punches: circle (4mm and 5mm), diamond (5mm), droplet (5mm)
- Rounded corner punch (optional)
- Pricking iron or stitching awl
- Wooden or rubber hammer, to use with leather punches and pricking iron
- Heavy-duty thread, waxed linen or nylon in a matching colour
- 2 heavy-duty sewing needles
- Rotary cutter and scissors
- Cutting mat
- Ruler (quilter's grid ruler, if available)
- Pen
- Removable tape
- Glue

The dimensions and template provided are for a 3rd and 4th generation iPad.

BEFORE YOU START

Photocopy and cut out the template on page 103. Transfer the template on the vegetable tanned leather and the nubuck. Note that the front has a cut-out near the top for easy grasp. Cut out with a rotary cutter, keeping the corners straight for now. The corners will be rounded after assembly (optional).

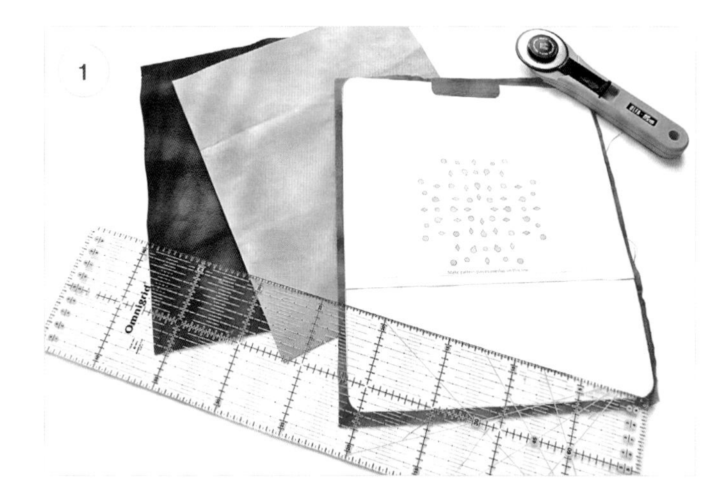

1 Using the same template, cut the fabric lining slightly bigger than the template. Do the same for the iron-on fabric adhesive but leave an open space on one of the two, where the cut-outs will be. Iron the adhesive to the wrong side of the fabric and put aside.

2 Cut out design: using removable tape, secure the template to the right side of the vegetable tan leather. Make sure you test a piece of scrap leather first to make sure the tape doesn't damage the leather when removing.

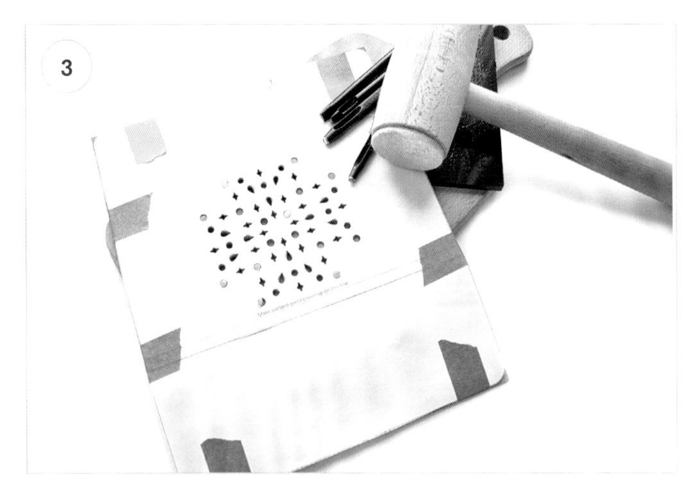

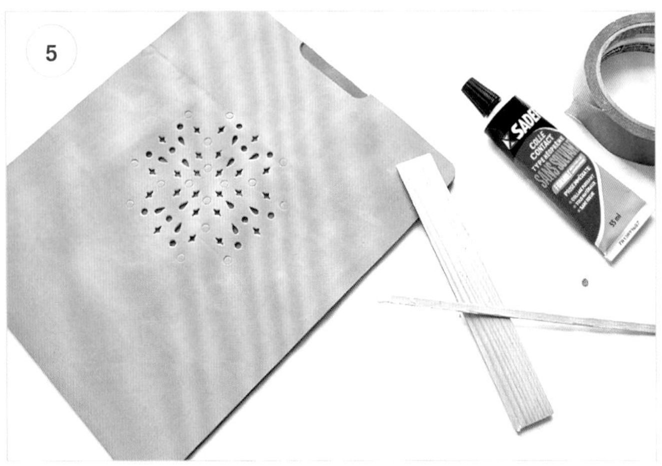

3 Using the corresponding punches and the wooden or rubber hammer, make the cut-out design in the leather, going through both paper and leather. Note that the cut-outs are made from the right side of the leather for a nicer result. Remove the template when finished.

4 Iron the fabric to the back of both pieces of leather (the one without glue in the middle goes on the back of the leather with the cutouts) and trim the excess fabric.

5 Apply a tiny bit of glue close to and all the way around the edge (except for the top) of one of the pieces of lined leather. Place the other piece on top and align. Leave to dry for a while. Using the rounded corner punch, round the corners. Trim edges where needed.

6 Using a stitching awl or pricking iron, make stitching holes about 1/8–1/4in (3mm–5mm) from the edge all the way around except for the top (opening). When using an awl, the size of the stitches shouldn't be any longer than about 1/8in (3mm–4mm).

7 Next, slip a needle to both ends of a long strand of sewing thread and sew the two pieces together using saddle stitch (see page 63). Finish with an overcast stitch and cut off the excess thread.

Tips

For extra softness, use an old t-shirt to line the cover. As an additional advantage, because a t-shirt is made of knitted fabric, it won't fray so easily.

You could also use the cut-out design template as a stencil: transfer the design onto freezer paper and make the cut-outs with a craft knife or scalpel. Iron the stencil onto the leather and apply paint. Leave to dry and peel off the stencil (do a test run first on a piece of scrap leather).

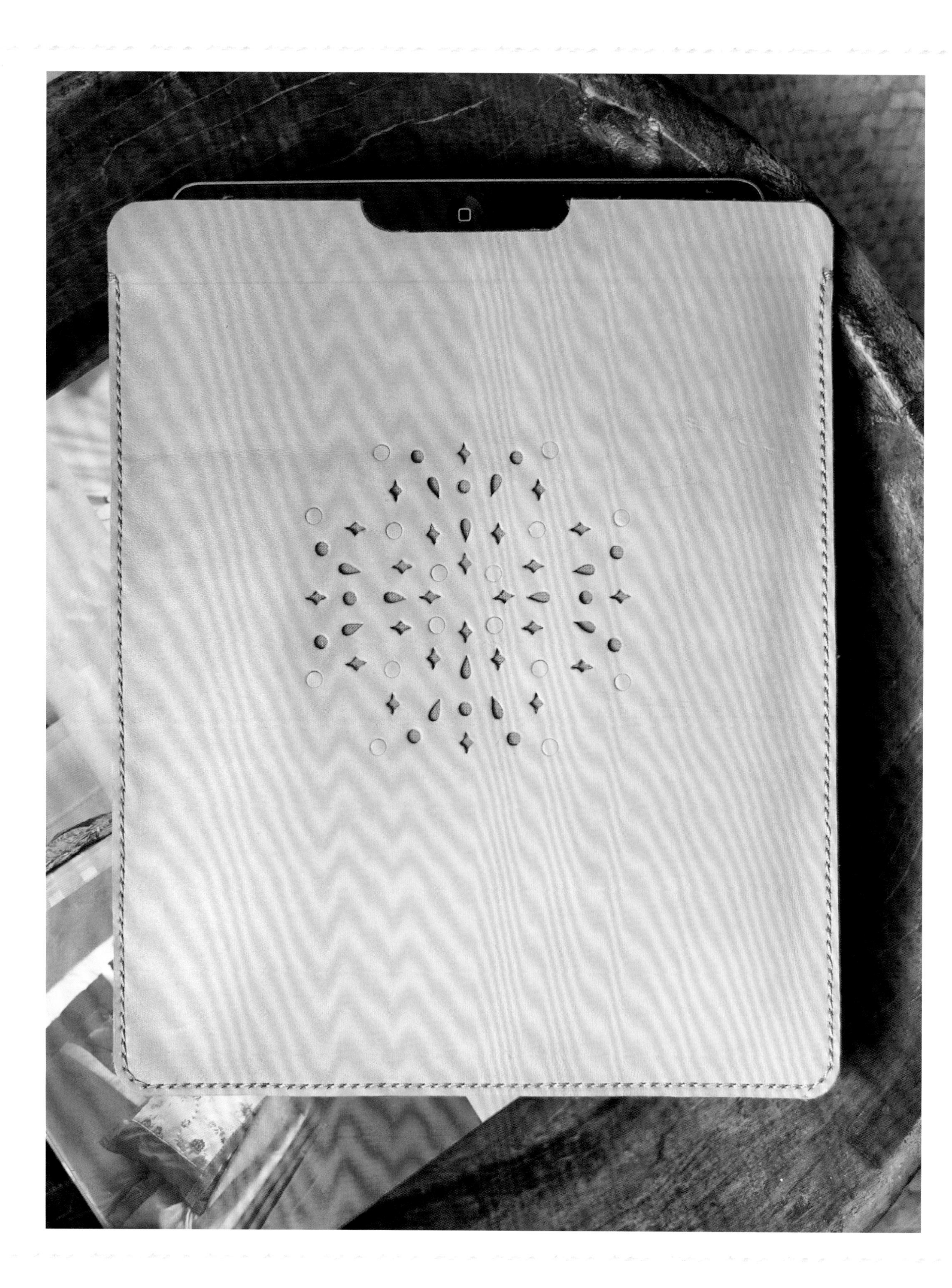

Do not include for front piece

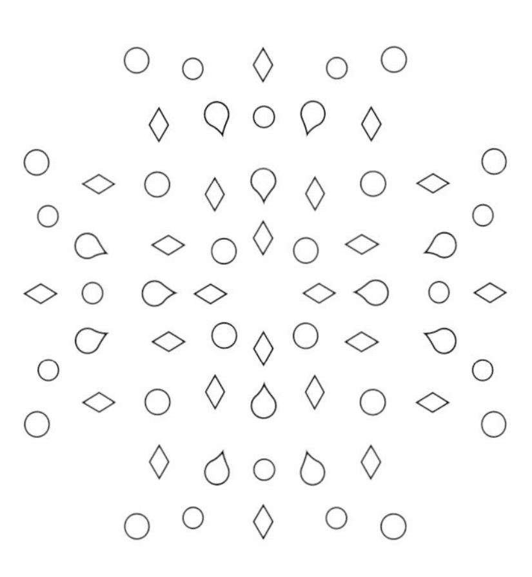

Photocopy at 200% for actual size

TEMPLATE

Jewellery basket

Keep your precious jewellery close to hand in this fancy and easy to make leather basket. Make separate ones for different types of jewellery if you wish.

Materials

- 8 x 8in (20 x 20cm) scrap leather
- 8½ x 8½in (22 x 22cm) fabric
- Iron-on fabric adhesive paper
- 2 rivets and a rivet setting tool
- Scissors
- Craft knife or rotary cutter with cutting mat
- Leather hole punch
- Iron
- Marker
- Ruler

BEFORE YOU START

Copy and cut out the template on page 108. Make holes in the paper template as indicated (four holes for the rivets and four holes to mark the base corners of the basket).

1 With a leather hole punch, make holes in the leather square as indicated. With a craft knife, make diagonal incisions in the leather along the cutting line as shown on the template, between each base corner hole and corresponding corner, cutting from hole to corner.

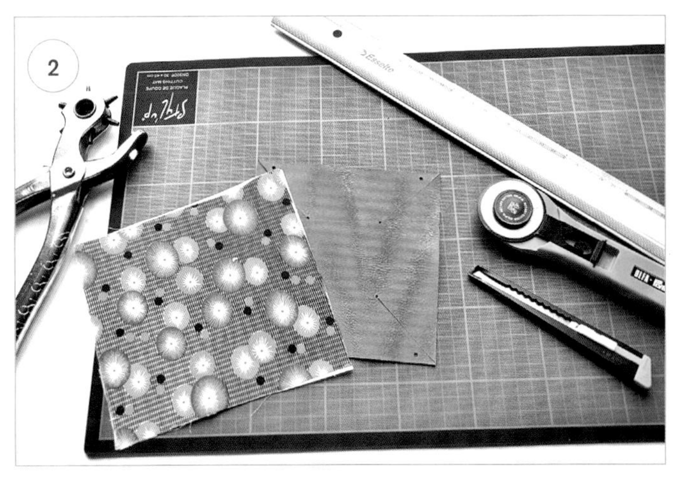

2 From the fabric and iron-on fabric adhesive paper, cut a square slightly bigger than the leather square. Iron the adhesive paper onto the wrong side of the fabric following the manufacturer's instructions.

3 Remove the paper backing. Iron the fabric to the wrong side of the leather square, making sure the leather isn't overlapping on the diagonals. Trim the excess fabric and cut the fabric on the diagonals following the incisions already in the leather (images 3 and 4).

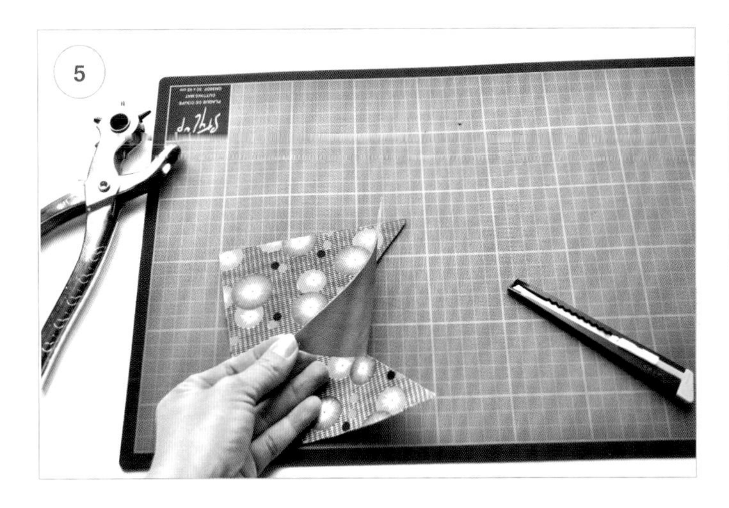

5 Join two opposing corners (A and D on the template) and set a rivet.

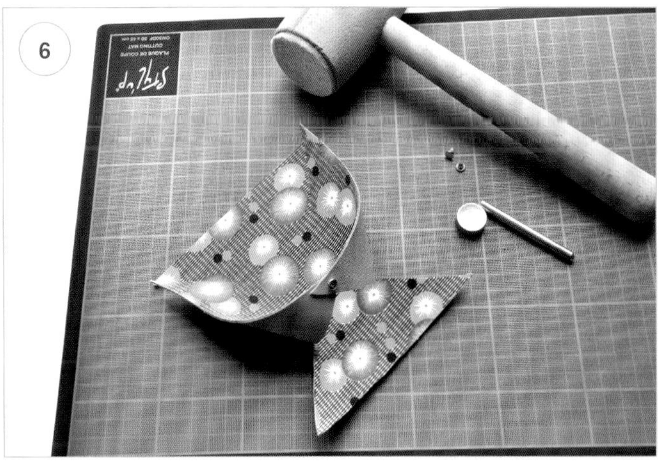

6 Repeat for the other set of corners (B and C on the template).

7 Shape the basket by inserting the remaining flaps (images 7 and 8).

Tips

Instead of rivets you could use snap closures, so you can undo the corners and store the basket flat.

When applying the fabric to the leather, make sure to iron on the fabric side, not on the leather side.

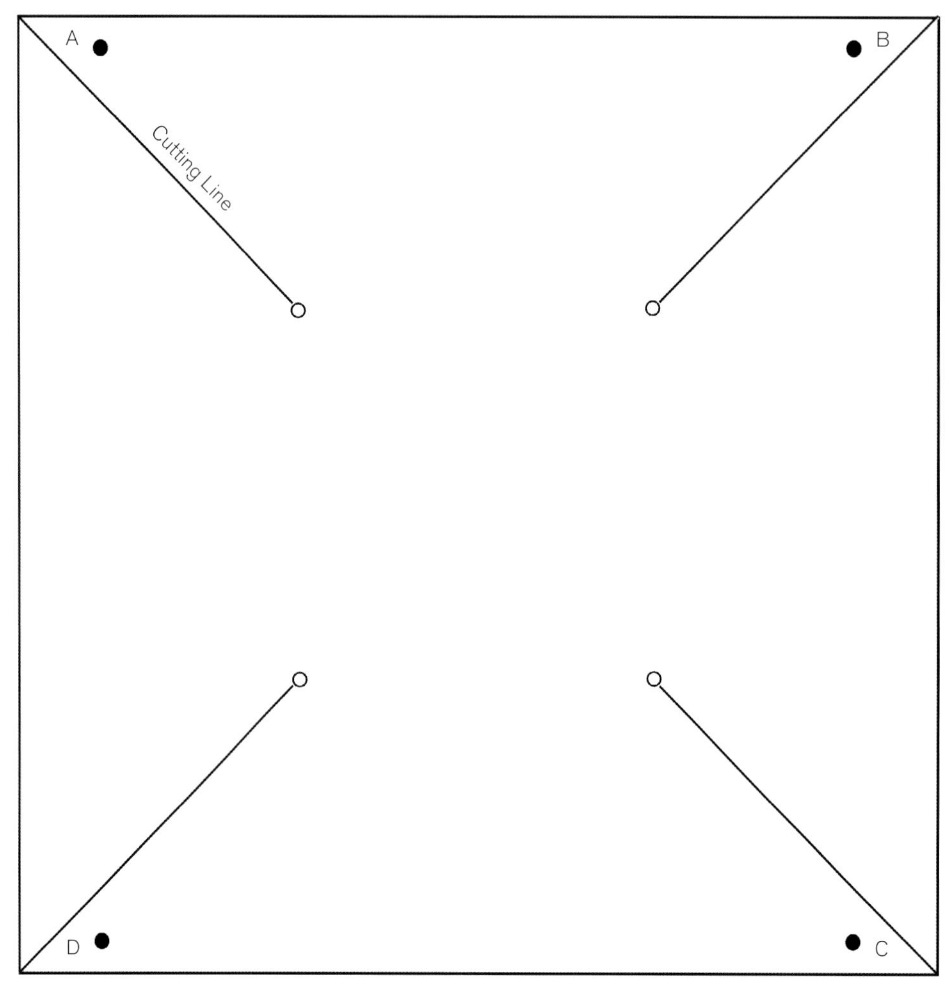

Photocopy at 125% for actual size

TEMPLATE

Woven belt chair

This is a great way to upcycle an old chair without having to upholster the seat.

Materials

- Leather belts
- Pliers
- Sandpaper
- Upholsterer's tacks
- Small hammer
- Scissors

1 Strip all seating from your chair – this one simply had a piece of plywood nailed to it. Use pliers to remove any old tacks and smooth down any rough wood with sandpaper.

2 Take a bit of time to lay out your belts, interweaving them, to decide what order and which parts of them to use.

3 Chair seats usually taper towards the back, so in order to get your spacing even, first lay one belt centrally from the front to the back of your chair. At this point consider which end of the belt to use – whether you want to incorporate the buckle holes or not.

4 Turning the chair upside down use three upholsterer's tacks in a triangular shape, to secure one end of the belt to the underside of the centre of the front of the seat. Trim the excess with scissors, to align with the inside edge of the seat's wooden frame.

5 Now working on the centre point of the back of the seat, pull the belt taut and secure it to the underside of the seat's frame with three more upholsterer's tacks as before. Again, trim any excess of the belt with scissors.

6 Now do the same with the central belt crossing your seat from side to side.

7 Working methodically, work from the central crossed belts outwards, weaving them in and out as you go to fill the seat area. Pull each belt as tight as you can as you work, and remember that the tapering shape of the seat will mean that the gaps between the belts will be smaller along the back of the seat.

Log basket

Keep wood dry and at the ready in this stylish but robust leather basket. This beautifully luxurious box bag is a great storage solution for firewood and kindling, and will look attractive in any fireside setting.

Materials

- 60in (1.5m) length of 55in (140cm) wide recycled leather fabric
- 60in (1.5m) length of 55in (140cm) wide natural linen (or similar), for lining
- Threads to match fabrics, plus a contrasting colour
- 60in (1.5m) very heavyweight stiffener
- 40in (1m) of ¾in (2cm) wide cotton tape
- Red waxed thread and leather needle
- Sewing machine
- Sewing needle
- Scissors
- Pins or clips
- Long ruler (40in/1m) and pen
- Brown paper/newspaper

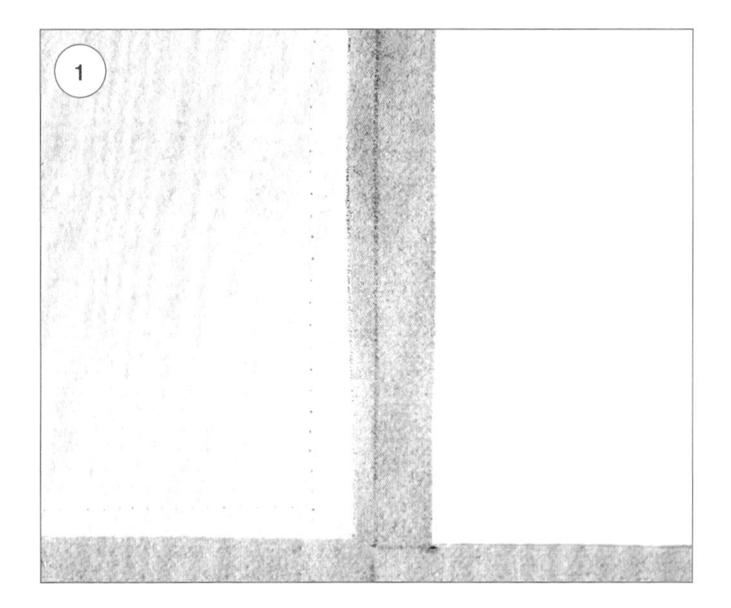

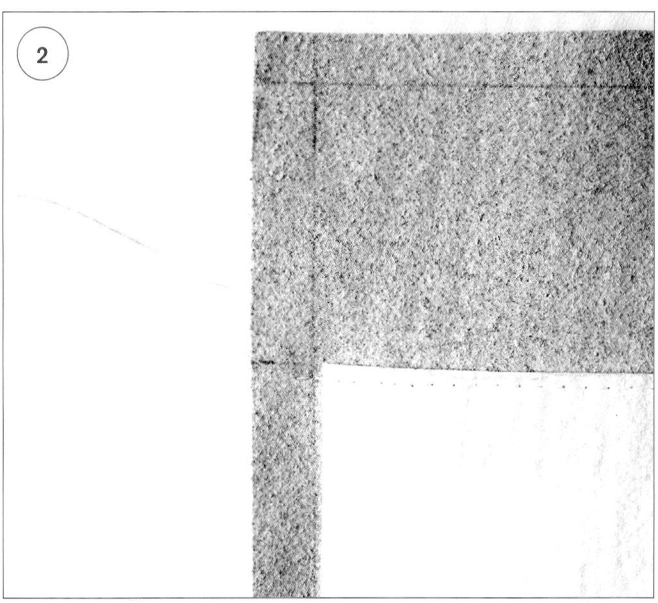

BEFORE YOU START

Use brown paper or newspaper to make the pattern (see page 117 for diagram). Cut one piece in leather fabric (black line) and one in linen (blue line). Cut three pieces of stiffener: one piece 19 x 19in (49 x 49cm) and two pieces 12 x 31½in (30 x 80cm).

1 Take the leather fabric first and lay face down. Lay the 19in (49cm) square of stiffener down, centred in the middle section. Use small bits of masking tape or pins to hold it in place before stitching the two layers together a few millimetres inside the edge of the stiffener.

2 Repeat with the two long pieces of stiffener, placing them 2½in (6cm) from the long outer edges, securing them with small pieces of tape and stitching them down along their two long edges only. Fold the leather fabric piece in half, wrong sides facing, across the narrowest section (see line on the diagram) and align all the raw edges. Stitch a ⅜in (1cm) seam along the 'A' edges.

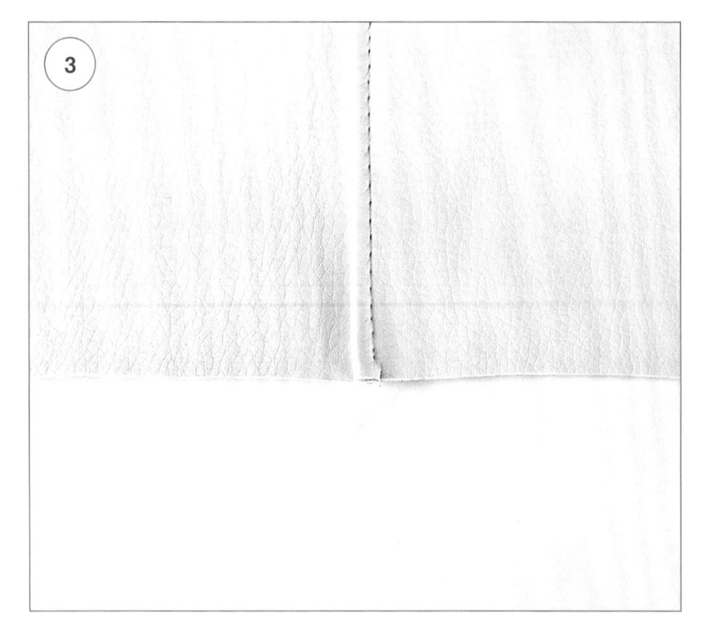

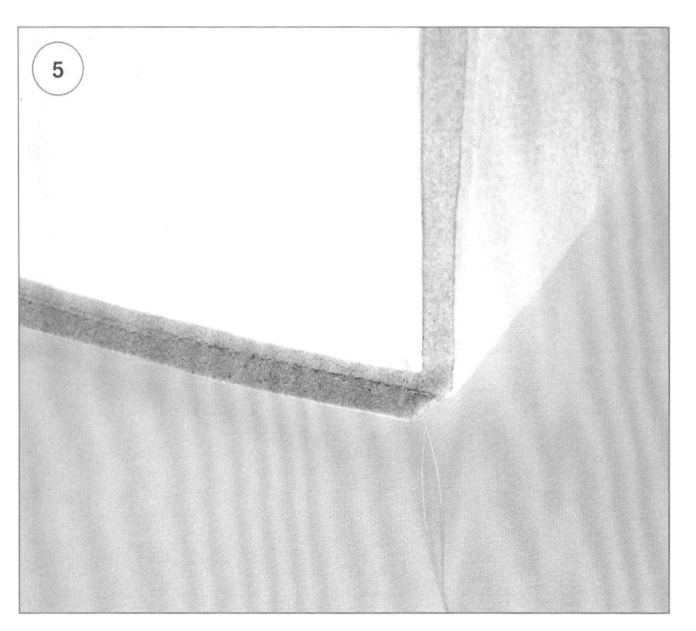

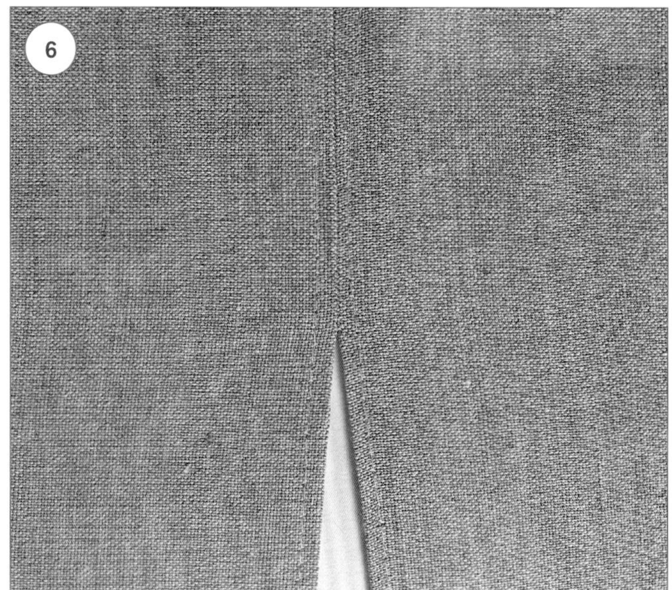

3 Push the seam to the left at the back of the work and stitch a line about ¼in (5mm) to the left of the seam through all layers. This can be a bit awkward – it's easier to do it from the right side, but with the work still inside out. Do the same with the 'B' edges.

4 With the work still inside out, flatten the one side seam so that it lies exactly along the centre fold of the base, right sides together. Pin or clip the raw edges together.

5 Stitch a ⅜in (1cm) seam to create a box corner. Repeat on the other side.

6 Take the lining linen. Cut along the centre fold line indicated on the template. Align the raw edges of the cut you've just made and pin them together. Stitch a ⅜in (1cm) seam 2in (5cm) in from each edge, thus leaving a turning gap. Press the seam and ⅜in (1cm) on either edge of the turning gap open. Machine sew along the folded edges of the turning gap to reinforce it.

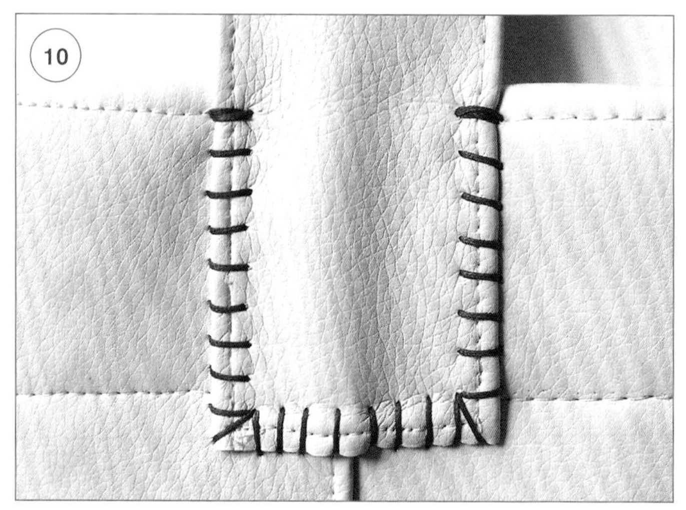

7 Align the 'A' and 'B' edges and stitch ⅜in (1cm) seams along them. Press open with a hot iron. Flatten the side seams and align with the central seam as you did in step 4. Stitch the two sides with ⅜in (1cm) seams to create the box corners. With the outer fabric still inside out, turn the lining right side out and lip it inside your outer piece. Align the top raw edges and side seams, pin or clip and sew a ⅜in (1cm) seam all the way around. Carefully ease the work through the turning gap to end up with the lining inside. Stitch the gap closed with small overstitches by hand. Fold the leather fabric just above the line of stitching from securing the stiffener at step 4 so that it folds over the top of the stiffener. Clip all the way around – I cushioned my clips with scraps of fabric to prevent them from bruising the leather fabric.

8 Stitch all the way around through the lining and the outer just below the join of the linen lining and the leather fabric. To make the handle, cut a length of leather fabric 5in (13cm) wide and 31½in (80cm) long. Fold it in half (now 2½in/6.5cm wide) with the length of tape sandwiched inside it along its length and protruding at either end. Stitch across one short end and the long edge.

9 Pull the tape at the open short end to turn the tube of fabric right side out.

10 Cut off the end attached to the tape. Flatten the tube of fabric out so that the seam runs centrally down one side. Topstitch approximately ¼in (6mm) in along either edge and across both short ends. Use red waxed thread and a leather needle or sharp tapestry needle to attach the handle to either side of the bag, centred on the side seams. Do three stitches on top of each other at the top on either side to add extra strength, plus a few stitches along the inside edge.

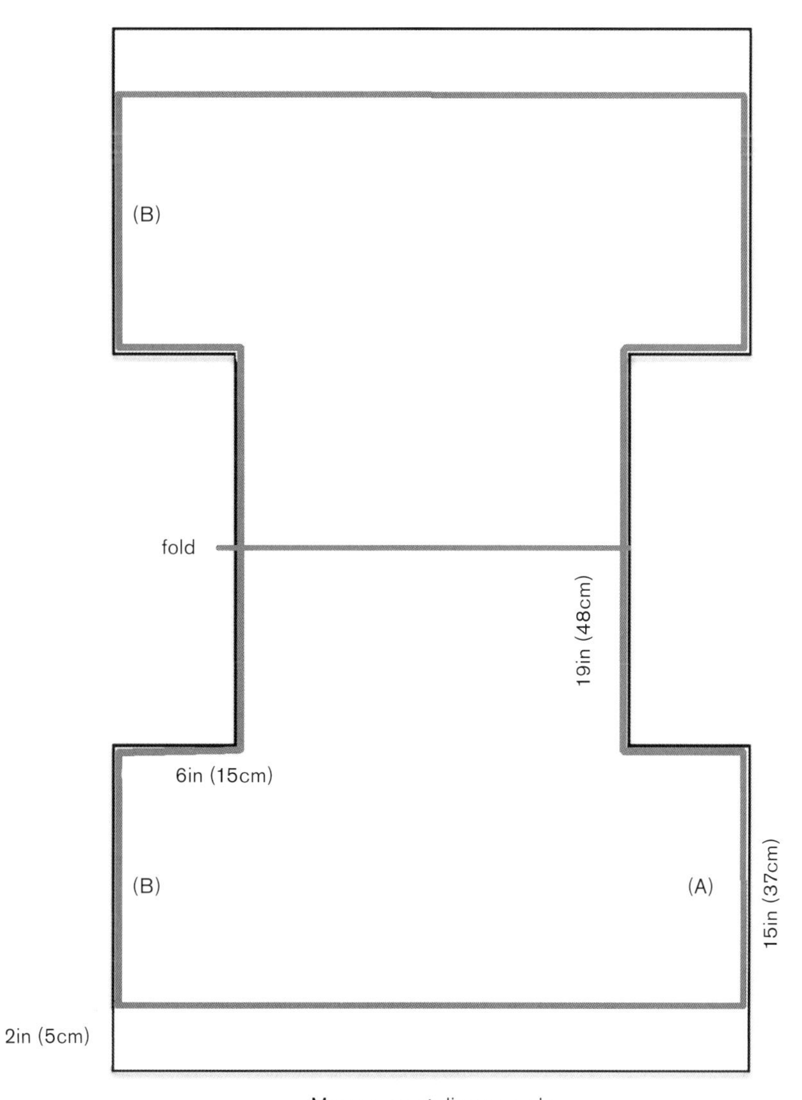

Measurement diagram only

Tips

Have a little practice with your sewing machine and the leather fabric – we found that a long stitch worked really well. The texture of the leather fabric can get slightly stuck to the bed of the machine, so use both hands to encourage it along under the foot as you stitch.

If you make mistakes, unpick the stitches – the leather fabric is fairly forgiving and stitch holes will generally close over to some extent and not show up much.

Resources

ART AND CRAFT SUPPLIES
Fred Aldous Ltd
37 Lever Street
Manchester
M1 1LW
Tel: +44 (0)161 236 4224
www.fredaldous.co.uk

Hobbycraft
(Stores nationwide)
Tel: +44 (0)330 026 1400
www.hobbycraft.co.uk

FAUX LEATHER, FRAMES, BAG-MAKING KITS
U-Handbag
30 Brunswick Street East
Hove
East Sussex
BN3 1AU
Tel: +44 (0)1273 748 944
www.u-handbag.com

JEWELLERY FINDINGS AND TOOLS
Cooksongold
59-83 Vittoria Street
Birmingham
B1 3NZ
Tel: +44 (0)121 200 2120
www.cooksongold.com

LEATHER BUCKLES, OFFCUTS, STRAPS, KITS AND ACCESSORIES
Simple Way
The Old Library
Derwent Street
Chopwell
Tyne and Wear
NE17 7HZ
Tel: +44 (0)1207 566 100
www.simpleway.co.uk

LEATHERCORD, CLASPS, BEADS AND WIRE
Beads Direct Ltd
Unit 10, Duke Street
Loughborough
Leicestershire
LE11 1ED
Tel: +44 (0)1509 218 028
www.beadsdirect.co.uk

LEATHERWORKING TOOLS, LEATHER AND LEATHERCRAFT SUPPLIES
Bowstock Ltd
6 Mill Lane
North Tawton
Devon
EX20 2EE
Tel: +44 (0)1837 820 77
www.bowstock.co.uk

Artisan Leather
(Online only)
www.artisanleather.co.uk

USA

LEATHERWORKING TOOLS, LEATHER AND LEATHERCRAFT SUPPLIES
Buckleguy.com
15 Graf Road
Newburyport
MA 01950
Tel: +1 978 213 9989
www.buckleguy.com

Weaver Leather, LLC
7540 CR 201
PO Box 68
Mt. Hope, Ohio 44660
Tel (toll free): +1 800 430 6278
www.weaverleathersupply.com

CRAFT SUPPLIES
Joann fabric and craft stores
(Stores nationwide)
Tel (toll free): +1 888 739 4120
www.joann.com

Michaels
(Stores nationwide)
Tel (toll free): +1 800 642 4235
www.michaels.com

AUSTRALIA

Crafts Online
PO Box 1040
Maroochydore QLD 4558
Tel: +61 1300 331 311
www.craftsonline.com.au

Birdsall Leathercraft
36 Chedwyn St
Botany
NSW 2019
Tel: +61 (0)2 9316 6299
www.birdsall-leather.com.au

Leffler
PO Box 1366
Kensington Road
Victoria
Tel: +61 1800 337 006
www.leffler.com.au

Acknowledgements

GMC would like to thank the following for their lovely designs:

Emma Herian Leaf belt, Purse and wallet; **Paula Fernandes** Drawstring pouch; **Pascale Mestdagh** Luggage tag, Coin purse, Hand-sewn bag, Fringed bag, No-sew pencil cases, Booklets, iPad cover, Jewellery basket; **Jemima Schlee** Daisy belt, Silk scarf belt, Key fobs, Belt purse, Punched leather purse, Clutch bag, Studded tote, Writing set, Woven belt chair, Log basket; **Jeanne Spaziani** Flower necklace, Rose brooch; **Clair Wolfe** Friendship bracelet, Glam rock necklace.

Index